The *Ultimate* ^ Guide for STUDENT PRODUCT Development &Evaluation

The *Ultimate* Guide ^ for STUDENT PRODUCT Development & Evaluation

Frances A. Karnes, Ph.D.
Kristen R. Stephens, Ph.D.

Copyright ©2000 Frances A. Karnes & Kristen R. Stephens
Graphic Production Libby Lindsey

ISBN 1-882664-57-4

PRUFROCK PRESS
P.O. Box 8813
Waco, TX 76714-8813
Phone: (800) 998-2208
Fax: (800) 240-0333
www.prufrock.com

Contents

LIST OF FIGURES

ACKNOWLEDGEMENTS

Thanks! Thanks! Thanks!

Special thanks are extended to all individuals and groups who have assisted in the process of making this a meaningful publication on product development and evaluation. Information was forwarded on the formulation of this book to many local, state, and national organizations that passed our request for information to their members through their newsletters, journals, and other publications. State consultants were helpful in seeking information on student products across the United States. We will always be indebted to the elementary and secondary youth who shared their ideas and products with us and to those adults who responded to our request for information and resources.

The staff at The Center for Gifted Studies has been very helpful in locating resources and in the preparation of the manuscript. Special mention must be made regarding the computer skills of Heather Ratliff and the management insights of Barbara VanDuser. Our reviewers: Kate Walker, Danell Napier, Jennifer Bochicchio, and Paul VanZandt, are to be commended as well. We continue to be grateful to the administrators at The University of Southern Mississippi for their support and enthusiasm for our publications.

We applaud our editor, Libby, and our publisher, Prufrock Press Inc., for recognizing the worth and usefulness of this publication and for acknowledging that no other book like this exists, thus making it the first to give a total overview of product development and evaluation for elementary and secondary students.

Our families have always been supportive of our efforts and accomplishments in publishing. Ray, John, Leighanne, and Mary Ryan Karnes, and David and Stephanie Stephens, along with Krystal and Katelyn continue to be sources of stability and love. The special guidance of Christopher Karnes and Karen Stephens will always be with us.

INTRODUCTION

Who Will Benefit From This Book

Elementary and secondary school students are the focus of this book. However, pre-schoolers and even perhaps college students will find this book helpful when creating products. Teachers at all levels and in all subjects can use the information in this book to help their students become exemplary product developers and evaluators. The number and variety of products will be of particular interest to parents and grandparents as they reflect on the work of their children and grandchildren in school and in the community. Guidance counselors, librarians, and media specialists will be able to make the information available to those seeking to expand their knowledge on the topic. Youth directors in all organizations will use this content to expand the ideas held by students on product development. As persons in business, the arts, sports, religious affiliations, and so forth develop links with schools and other groups, they will welcome this information on product development to meet the unique needs of the students who are of the greatest interest to them. Share this book with all the previously mentioned groups as well as with friends, relatives, and other important students and adults in your life.

How Products Were Selected for This Book

The products selected for this book focusing on elementary and secondary students were gleaned from many sources and divided into the following topics: visual, oral, performance, written, and multi-categorical. The intent was to be all-encompassing and to include as many products as possible within each category. Much time and effort has been given to locate all products that could be developed by the target groups. As with all human endeavors, a few may have been overlooked, and those should be added to the corresponding areas.

How to Use This Book

The book is easy to use and has been divided into 10 chapters. Chapter I contains general information on products: definitions; products listed in the areas of visual, oral, written, performance, and multi-categorical; what you should know about their development; and the benefits of creating them. Chapter II provides information on getting started in the development of products, including the formulation of a topic, organization of product aspects, the transformation of content into products, the art and science of communication through them, and the extremely necessary component of evaluation. The creation of rubrics for the latter is described, and examples are given in Chapter III.

Chapter IV, V, VI, VII, and VIII focus on visual, oral, performance, written, and multi-categorical products, respectively. In each of these chapters, a multitude of information is provided: description of the product type, and information on the specific product, which includes a definition, title of the expert, the specific types, words to know, helpful hints, exemplary producers, community resources, and quotes to inspire. Examples of rubrics are also provided, as well as students' stories of how they developed certain products, and a listing of other products in each category. Each chapter concludes with web sites, software, and a bibliography of books for additional information. Chapter IX has other useful ideas on how to use products in competitions with examples of a few at the national level.

A product journal concludes the book, providing the opportunity for reflection on product development. A form is also given for you to share your product ideas with us. We look forward to hearing from you.

CHAPTER 1

What is a Product?

A product is tangible evidence of what has been learned through study and investigation. When a fifth-grade girl studies the implications of traffic patterns in the community, she may want to display her new knowledge by one or all of the following: writing an editorial for the local newspaper, creating a video to be displayed in the mall, or developing a document to be shared with the director of transportation for the city. After looking into the accomplishments of Abraham Lincoln, a seventh-grade boy wrote a script, created a stage set, and delivered a monologue to various groups of children and adults. These are but a few examples of how facts and figures can be transformed into interesting products to be shared with a variety of persons within the school and community.

Products! Products! Products!

There are many different types of products: written, oral, visual, performance, and multi-categorical. A listing of possible products appears on the opposite page. Perhaps you can think of others!

Factors to be Considered in Product Development

There are many factors to consider when making a decision on the development of a specific type of product. The content may expand or limit the options, but most products are adaptable to all subject areas. Additionally, the learning styles of individuals vary and should be considered. For students with advanced art skills, visual products may be the area in which to get started. For those with outstanding writing abilities, products within the written category could be a beginning point. After a comfort level is achieved with beginning products, other styles should be examined to make and meet more challenges within product development.

Other circumstances should also be considered, such as the audience with whom the product will be shared. A multimedia presentation on the topic of recycling for a better environment would be more appropriate for older students and adults, while a puppet show would be great to hold the attention of younger students. Another factor to consider in product development is the availability of materials. Are all readily available? Can they be obtained in the time necessary to develop the type of product you want to create? For example, a multimedia slide show may be more time consuming to design than a poster. Mobility of the product is also a consideration with audiences outside of the school. A large diorama or model is not easily transported to multiple locations.

Figure 1: Types of Products

Abstract	Cookbook	Graph	Menu	Political Cartoon	Slide Show
Acronym	Cooked Concoction	Graphic	Metaphor	Pop-Up Book	Sociogram
Activity Sheet	Costume	Graphic Organizer	Mini Center	Portfolio	Song
Advertisement	Crest	Greeting Card	Mobile	Position Paper	Speech
Alphabet Book	Critique	Guest Speaker	Mock Trial	Poster	Spreadsheet
Animation	Cross Section	Guide	Model	Prediction	Stage Setting
Annotated Bibliography	Crossword Puzzle	Handbook	Monologue	Presentation	Stained Glass
Aquarium	Dance	Hidden Picture	Monument	Program	Stencil
Archive	Database	Histogram	Montage	Project Cube	Stitchery
Art Gallery	Debate	Hologram	Motto	Puppet	Story
Autobiography	Demonstration	How to Book	Multimedia Presentation	Puppet Show	Story Board
Banner	Design	Hypermedia	Mural	Questionnaire	Summary
Bibliography	Diagram	Hypothesis	Museum	Quilt	Survey
Big Book	Dialogue	Illusion	Musical Composition	Quotation	Table
Biography	Diary	Illustrated Story	Musical Instrument	Radio Show	Tape Recording
Blueprint	Dictionary	Illustration	Musical Performance	Rap	Television Show
Board Game	Diorama	Index Cards	Mystery	Rebus Story	Terrarium
Book	Display	Instructions	Narrative	Recipe	Tessellation
Book Jacket	Document	Internet Search	Newsletter	Recitation	Test
Book Review	Documentary	Interview	Newspaper	Reenactment	Textbook
Broadcast	Dramatization	Invention	Novel	Relief Map	Theory
Brochure	Drawing	Investigation	Origami	Report	Three-D Model
Budget	Editorial	Itinerary	Oral Report	Riddle	Time Capsule
Bulletin Board	Equation	Jewelry	Organization	Role Play	Timeline
Bumper Sticker	Essay	Jigsaw Puzzle	Outline	Routine	Trademark
Business Plan	Etching	Jingle	Overhead Transparency	Rubber Stamp	Travelogue
Button	Evaluation Checklist	Journal	Packet	Rubbing	Triptych
Campaign	Event	Kit	Painting	Rubric	Venn Diagram
Cartoon	Exhibit	Laser Show	Pamphlet	Samples	Video
Carving	Experiment	Learning Center	Panel Discussion	Sand Casting	Video Game
Celebration	Fact File	Lecture	Pantomime	Scavenger Hunt	Vocabulary List
Chart	Fairy Tale	Lesson	Paper Mache	Scenario	Wall Hanging
Club	Family Tree	Letter	Pattern	Science Fiction Story	Weaving
Coat of Arms	Field Experience	Limerick	Performance	Scrapbook	Webbing
Collage	Film	List	Personal Experience	Script	Web Page
Collection	Flag	Literary Analysis	Photo Album	Sculpture	Woodworking
Coloring Book	Flannel Board Story	Log	Photo Essay	Self-Portrait	Word Puzzle
Comedy Skit	Flip Book	Logic Puzzle	Photograph	Seminar	Written Paper
Comic Strip	Flow Chart	Logo	Photo Journalism	Service Project	
Commemorative Stamp	Flyer	Machine	Pictograph	Shadow Box	
Commentary	Folder Game	Magazine	Pictorial Essay	Shadow Play	
Commercial	Fractal	Magazine Article	Picture Dictionary	Short Story	
Competition	Game	Magic Show	Picture Story	Sign	
Computer Document	Game Show	Manual	Pie Chart	Silk Screening	
Computer Program	Geodesics	Map with Key	Plan	Simulation	
Conference Presentation	Geometric Model	Mask	Play	Sketch	
Construction	Glossary	Matrix	Poem	Skit	

(Karnes & Stephens, 2000)

2

Benefits From Creating Products

Many times, the demonstration of what has been learned is assessed through paper and pencil tests. Designing and developing products goes way beyond this method and combines much more, such as advanced content, process skills, and organizational aspects. One or all areas of content can be combined into product development: language arts, social studies, mathematics, arts, technology, and others. Process skills will be developed, such as oral and written communication skills; creativity and creative problem solving; the higher order thinking skill of analysis, synthesis, and evaluation; social and personal skills; and scientific and library research skills. Also, with each new product created, the organizational skills of planning, record keeping, and time management will be enhanced. When working with others, the aspects of group dynamics, such as teamwork, decision making, communication, and creative problem solving, can be further developed.

CHAPTER II

What Do You Want to Learn More About?

The possibilities of topics to research are limitless. Consider your interests and hobbies when choosing a topic, and select an area in which you are genuinely interested in learning. Remember, the more fascinating your selected topic, the more you will enjoy the research process.

There are several things to consider before choosing a topic to research. First, it is important to select a topic on which new knowledge can be acquired. For example, if you have already completed several in-depth research projects on tornadoes, it might be best to choose a new topic for which you are not already familiar. Keep in mind, topics can be found across all fields and subject areas. In addition, some topics may be content-related while others may represent a concept. Below is a sample listing of both content- and concept-related topics that could be explored. Can you think of others?

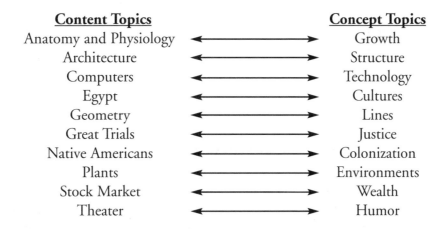

Content Topics		**Concept Topics**
Anatomy and Physiology	←——→	Growth
Architecture	←——→	Structure
Computers	←——→	Technology
Egypt	←——→	Cultures
Geometry	←——→	Lines
Great Trials	←——→	Justice
Native Americans	←——→	Colonization
Plants	←——→	Environments
Stock Market	←——→	Wealth
Theater	←——→	Humor

In order to give the research focus, it may be necessary to narrow broad-based topics down to smaller, more specific subtopics. For example, astronomy may be too large a subject to cover adequately, but it can be narrowed into such subtopics as black holes, comets, Venus, and the Milky Way Galaxy. Constructing a webbing, such as the one in Figure 2, can assist in this process.

Figure 2: Sample Webbing

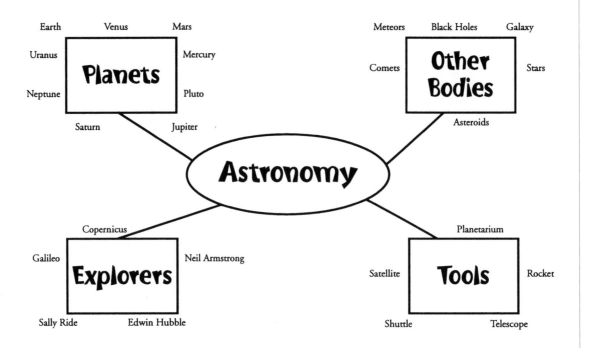

Research! Research! Research!

Once a topic is selected, it is time to begin the research process. Before beginning, a series of research readiness activities is essential. Research readiness is a term referring to the organizational activities that precede the research process. These activities might include generating a list of questions pertaining to the topic and producing a list of resources in which the answers to these formulated questions might be found. Such planning will assist in guiding your research. Furthermore, the development of a What I Know—What I Want to Know—What I Learned Chart (KWL) like the one in Figure 3 may also be beneficial during this stage of product development.

Figure 3: KWL Chart for Rainforests

Know	Want to Know	Learned
• There is a lot of rain.	• What are some specific animals that live in rainforests?	• Hercules beetles, the Lemadophis snake, Atta ants, Atelopus, frogs, bats, hummingbirds, jaguars, agoutis, anteaters, parrots, and howler monkeys are a a few of the animals that live in the rainforest.
• Some are located in South America.	• What is being done to help save rainforests?	
• They are being destroyed.	• How much rain do they have each year?	• Rainforests are also found in Asia.
• A variety of animals live in the rainforests.	• What other parts of the world have rainforests?	• Native Indians live in the rainforests of South America. They make their clothing and shelter from rainforests plants and animals.
	• Do people live in rainforests?	

It is also advisable to select a topic for which resources are available. Resources that can be used to gather information relating to your topic include:

Periodicals
    Journal
    Magazine
    Newsletter
    Newspaper

Books
    Content-Specific
    Encyclopedia
    Manual
    Reference

Audio-Visual Media
    Cassette Recording
    CD-ROM
    Film Strip

Television Program
Internet
Video

Miscellaneous
    Authentic Documents
    Letter
    Report
    Meeting/Symposium
    Dissertation/Thesis
    Monograph
    E-mail
    Memo
    Personal Communication
    Unpublished Manuscript

What Type of Product Do You Want to Create?

Deciding on a type of product to display the knowledge gained from the topic can be a difficult task. Kettle, Renzulli, and Rizza (1998) have devised *My Way … An Expression Style Inventory*. This instrument can be used to gather information about the types of products that you may be interested in creating. This inventory divides products into 10 different categories: written, oral, artistic, computer, audio-visual, commercial, service, dramatization, manipulative, and musical. By answering a series of questions on a Likert-type scale, it can be determined which sort of product would most interest you. Other ways to select a product type might be accomplished by completing an interest inventory or generating a list of hobbies and strengths.

While it is important to choose a product type that is intriguing, other circumstances must also be considered before selecting a product. For example, what are the characteristics of the audiences for whom the final product will be shared? While a song may be appropriate to inform younger audiences about the necessity of recycling, it may not be suitable for convincing community leaders. In addition, considering which type of product is best suited to display the selected subject matter is crucial. For instance, you will have to decide whether a graph, diorama, play, multimedia slide show, or another product would best display the stages of metamorphosis. While all may be appropriate, decide which one would be best suited to convey the newly acquired knowledge to the selected audience.

In addition to the above considerations, remember to be adventurous in selecting a product. Try your hand at creating a variety of different kinds of products. If you have designed several posters or written many stories in the past, why not try something new? Strengths and skills can be incorporated in an array of products, so expand your horizons. Figure 4 provides a way to keep a record of the types of products developed. This form can be carried with students as they advance across grade levels.

Figure 4

Student Product Inventory

Student: _____

Date	Type of Product	Academic Subject	Grade Level/Teacher

Methods for Planning and Organizing

Careful planning is essential before beginning the research process. The first step is to create a time line and determine an estimated date of completion. Be reasonable with the deadlines set. For example, some products may require more time to construct, or certain selected topics may demand a longer period to research. Prior to beginning, estimate which stages of product development will require the most time and plan accordingly. Furthermore, if certain process stages take longer than originally estimated, it may be necessary to revise completion dates along the way. However, by initially establishing deadlines, product production will be kept on track.

The next step is to generate a list of materials that are needed in order to complete the proposed product. Be aware that accommodations may need to be made for certain materials, due to their expense and availability. Use a little creative problem solving if certain items need to be substituted for others. In addition, be prepared that some materials may not work as initially intended, and adaptations and experimentation with other types of media may be required. In order to ensure that you have a supply of various materials on hand, it is advisable to send a list such as the one in Figure 5 home so that parents, grandparents, and friends can donate such items.

Another suggestion is to keep a daily log of progress to assist in planning activities from day to day. For example, record accomplishments each day and plan activities for the next day's work ahead of time. By thinking in advance, determinations can be made about any necessary materials or resources that may be needed to achieve future goals. Also, by having a daily agenda, product production is guided toward the estimated date of completion. Figure 6 provides an example of information that may be kept in a daily log.

Figure 5

Don't Throw It Away!

Egg and Milk Cartons
Cans (Coffee, Soup, etc.)
Aluminum Foil
Fabric Scraps
Buttons
Spools
Plastic Berry Baskets
Boxes (Shoe, Jewelry, etc.)
Microwave Meal Trays
Butter Tubs
Ribbon
Wrapping Paper

Toilet Paper Tubes
Paper Towel Tubes
Wire Coat Hangers
Packaging Popcorn
Nuts, Bolts, Screws
Colored Paper Scraps
Greeting Cards
Old Magazines
Newspapers
Clothespins
Yarn/String
Broken Costume Jewelry
Beads

CHAPTER III

Creating Rubrics to Evaluate Products

Before beginning to develop your product, it is important to establish criteria specific to the product on which it will be evaluated. The product grids found in the following chapters are a good place to begin. Also, consulting with an expert in the topic or product field may be useful in developing a list of components and exemplary characteristics for the proposed product. For example, a cartographer or a geography professor would be an excellent resource for assistance in producing a map, while an architect would be most helpful in designing a blueprint. For additional ideas, see the community resources listed for each product profiled in Chapters IV through VIII of this book or those listed in Figure 9. Remember, experts can be found everywhere. Some suggestions for where to find experts are offered in Figure 10.

Figure 9

Ask an Expert!

Blueprint/Architect
Brochure/Marketing Consultant
Debate/Speech-Debate Teacher
Experiment/Scientist
Family Tree/Genealogist
Magazine/Editor
Musical Composition/
   Music Professor

Photograph/Photographer
Play/Actor or Professor of Theater
Web Page/Computer Expert
Sculpture/Local Artist
Exhibit/Museum Curator
Map/Cartographer—Geography
   Department

Figure 10

 # Where Can You Dig Up Experts?

Colleges/Universities
Businesses
Your Community
Clubs & Organizations
Ask a Friend

Craft Guilds
Local Media
The Internet
The Library

From the selected criteria a rubric can be constructed. A rubric is a framework for evaluating products on an established scale. Begin by listing the components of the proposed product. For example, if the product is a poster, the components might include: title, labels, graphics, and layout. The next step would be to write exemplary characteristics for each component as follows:

Components	Characteristics
Title	• Legible; Neat • Prominent; Visible • Representative of Topic; Appropriate • Correct Spelling/Grammar
Labels	• Legible; Neat • Appropriate Placement • Correct Spelling/Grammar
Graphics	• Clear; Visible • Appropriate to Theme • Securely Attached
Layout	• Balanced • Non-Cluttered • Interesting • Appropriate Emphasis

After characteristics have been listed for each component of the product, it is time to set the scoring criteria or scale for each characteristic. When deciding on a scale, it is important to provide ratings for each characteristic. Care should be taken in avoiding odd numbered evaluation scales; a four- or a six-point scale is recommended. With odd numbered scales there is a tendency for the rater to select the middle value. In addition, each level of production should be defined to illustrate what it represents. For example, a "1" may be designated as "Poor" or "Incomplete," while a "4" may represent "Outstanding," "Superior," or "Top Notch" production. Figure 11 is an example of a completed rubric that was created by following the above steps. Furthermore, ready-made rubrics can be found in many books and on various Internet sites. Care should be taken in adapting such rubrics to meet your specific needs. A listing of such resources is provided at the conclusion of this chapter.

Figure 11: Sample Rubric for a Poster

Components	Characteristics	Ratings
Title	• Legible; Neat • Prominent; Visible • Representative of Topic; Appropriate • Correct Spelling/Grammar	1 2 3 4 5 6 1 2 3 4 5 6 1 2 3 4 5 6 1 2 3 4 5 6
Labels	• Legible; Neat • Appropriate Placement • Correct Spelling/Grammar	1 2 3 4 5 6 1 2 3 4 5 6 1 2 3 4 5 6
Graphics	• Clear; Visible • Appropriate to Theme • Securely Attached	1 2 3 4 5 6 1 2 3 4 5 6 1 2 3 4 5 6
Layout	• Balanced • Non-Cluttered • Interesting • Appropriate Emphasis	1 2 3 4 5 6 1 2 3 4 5 6 1 2 3 4 5 6 1 2 3 4 5 6

1 = Incomplete   4 = Emerging
2 = Needs Improvement   5 = Good
3 = Fair   6 = Superior

References

Books

Ainsworth, L., & J. Christinson (1998). *Student-generated rubrics: An assessment model to help all students succeed.* Palo Alto, CA: Dale Seymour Publications.

Flagg, A. (1999). *Rubrics, checklists & other assessments for science you teach: Easy assessments to use with your favorite science activities.* New York: Scholastic Professional Book Division.

Lazear, D. (1998). *The rubric way: Using MI to assess understanding.* Tucson, AZ: Zephyr Press.

Rickards, D. (1998). *Designing rubrics for K–6 Classroom.* Norwood, MA: Christopher-Gordon Publishing.

Taggart, G. L. (Eds.) (1998). *Rubrics: A guide for construction and use in the school setting.* Lancaster, PA: Technomic Publishing Co.

Wiggins, G. P. (1998). *Educative assessment: Designing assessments to inform and improve student performance.* San Francisco: Jossey-Bass Publishers.

Web sites

http://edweb.sdsu.edu/triton/July/rubrics/Rubrics_for_Web_Lessons.html
Creating Rubrics

http://edweb.sdsu.edu/triton/tidepoolunit/Rubrics/reportrubric.html
Scientific Report Rubric

http://edweb.sdsu.edu/triton/tidepoolunit/Rubrics/collrubric.html
Collaboration Rubric

http://memorial.sdcs.k12.ca.us/LESSONS/WWII/WWIIunit/HyperStudiorubric.html
Hyperstudio Project Rubric

http://memorial.sdcs.k12.ca.us/LESSONS/WWII/WWIIunit/writfirst.html
Rubric for Firsthand Biography

http://memorial.sdcs.k12.ca.us/LESSONS/WWII/WWIIunit/oralpresentation.html
Oral Presentation Rubric

http://edweb.sdsu.edu/triton/july/Rubric_Guidelines.html
Guidelines for Rubric Development

http://edweb.sdsu.edu/triton/july/Rubric_Template.html
Rubric Template

http://sltech.com/Product.html
The Rubricator

http://horizon.nmsu.edu/ddl/portfoliorub.html
Portfolio Scoring Rubric

http://www.cs.ius.indiana.edu/AK/JROSE/WEB_DOCS/vidrub.htm
Video Critique Rubric

http://www.sv400.k12.ks.us/tips/webpagerubric.html
Web Page Design Rubric

http://ais.cs.sandia.gov/AiS/manual/eval/research_rubric.html
Research Rubric

http://etr-associates.org/nsrc/rcv2n4/rubric.html
Rubrics: An Assessment Tool To Share with Students

http://ac.grin.edu:80/~hunterj/forum/WFV33gradingrubric.html
Grading Criteria for Academic Papers

http://athena.wednet.edu/curric/weather/adptcty/assess2.html
Group Participation Assessment Rubric

http://sun.kent.wednet.edu/KSD/KR/ScienceDept/subjects/physicspages/port.rubric.html
Scoring Rubric for Portfolio Exhibits, Power Presentation, and for Portfolios

http://www.learningspace.org/instruct/lessons/pst4.html
Multimedia Grading Rubric

http://georgew.gw.pps/pgh.pa.us/rubrics/hprubric.html
Scoring Rubric for Student Homepage Projects

CHAPTER IV

Visual Products

Visual products are those that communicate ideas and knowledge through a variety of media and emphasize sight and space as the primary mode of learning. Visual products include but are not limited to:

Advertisement	Graph
Bar Graph	Illustration
Blueprint	Map
Book Jacket	Mobile
Brochure	Mural
Bullet Chart	Pie Chart
Bulletin Board	Poster
Cartoon	Storyboard
Collage	Story Map
Concept Cube	Time line
Cross-Section	Tree Chart
Drawing	Venn Diagram
Flow Chart	Webbing

This chapter contains in-depth profiles of 13 selected visual products. Information such as product definitions, title of experts, types, words to know, helpful hints, exemplary producers, community resources, and quotes to inspire are provided. These listings can be expanded as you begin your research and development of your products. In addition, product grids follow comprising the components, characteristics, and basic materials of each profiled product. Examples of authentic student products are also highlighted. Concluding this chapter is a useful bibliography of selected books, web sites, and software helpful in creating specific visual products.

Product: Cartoon

Definition: A drawing, often humorous, that presents a complete thought.

Title of Expert: Cartoonist

Types of Cartoons:

Animated	Narrative Art
Comic Strip	Political
Editorial	Single Panel
Gag Panel	Sport

Words to Know:

Balloon	Lettering
Caption	Panel
Caricature	Pencils
Composition	Perspective
Drawing Board	Proportion
Humor	Sarcasm
Illustration	Syndicate
Ink	Tracing Paper

Helpful Hints:

- Never be satisfied with the first idea that comes to you.
- Keep the focus on the foreground; do not divert attention to details in the background.
- Sketch in pencil first, then follow with ink.
- Draw your material from real-life situations.
- Balloon conversation must be familiar, informal, simple, and direct so the reader can understand.
- Make every word count.
- Hold the appearance of the character from drawing to drawing.
- Don't worry about technique; it will develop.
- Vary the shape of the head, nose, ears, eyes, mouth, and hair to add to facial expressions.
- Get a good anatomy book and keep it on hand.

Exemplary Producers:

Scott Adams	Etta Hulme
Charles Samuel Addams	Henry King Ketcham
Donna Armento	Walter Crawford Kelly
Peter Arnod	Harvey Kurtzman

George Baker
Walter Bendt
Randy Bisson
Herbert Lawrence Block
George Booth
Berke Breathed
Al Capp
George Criones
Jim Davis
Walt Disney
Jules Feiffer
Rube Goldberg
Chester Gould
Cathy Guisewife
Harold Lincoln Gray
William Gropper
Bill Hoest
Helen Elna Hokinson

Gary Larson
William Henry Maudlin
Otto Mesmer
Thomas Nast
Kate Palmer
Charles Schulz
Bill Seelback
Elzie Crisler Segar
Joseph Shuster
Jerry Siegel
Saul Steinberg
Sir John Tenniel
David Thorne
James Grover Thurber
Gary Trudeau
Larry Wright
Murat Bernard Young

Community Resources: Art Teacher, Artist, Local Cartoonist, Newspaper Editor

Quotes to Inspire:

"A drawing is always dragged down to the level of its caption."

—James Thurber

"The most perfect caricature is that which, on a small surface, with the simplest means, most accurately exaggerates, to the highest point, the peculiarities of a human being, at his most characteristic moment in the most beautiful manner."

—Sir Max Beerbohm

Product Criteria Grid

Product: Cartoon

Components	Characteristics	Basic materials
Title (optional)	• Relevant to situation/topic, attracts reader's attention, original	Colored Pencils Eraser India Ink Markers Paper Ruler Tracing Paper
Situation/Topic	• Reflective of current events, familiar to intended audience	
Drawing/Caricature	• Representative of the situation/person in question, self-explicit, easy to understand, timely, neat	
Caption (optional)	• Concise, humorous, use of appropriate grammar and spelling, neat, legible	
Humor (optional)	• Appropriate for intended audience, universal, significant to the events of the time	

Product: Carving

Definition: The art of manipulating material with a sharp instrument into a desired object or form, either realistic or abstract.

Title of the Expert: Carver, Woodworker

Types of Carvings:

Cameo	Masks
Chip	Petroglyph
Clay	Pierced
Etching	Plaster
Figurehead	Relief
Glyptograph	Scrimshaw
Intaglio	Totem Pole
Jack O'Lantern	Wax
Marble	

Words to Know:

Adze	Kerf-Cut
Awl	Knife
Band Saw	Levering
Blank	Mallet
Burin	Marquette
Chisel	Netsuke
Clamp	Sanding
Drawknife	Scroll Saw
Engrave	Stop-Cut
Glyptic	Stropping
Gouge	Trenching
Grindstone	Veiner Tool
Holdfast	Vise
Honing	V-Tool
Incised	Whittle
Inscription	

Helpful Hints:

- Remember that different knives are used for different tasks.
- Work on a thick, heavy, and sturdy surface that is an appropriate height.
- Keep your tools sharp and in order.
- If carving wood, select your type and piece of wood carefully.

- Know the basic holds before beginning.
- Plan your project before beginning.
- Decide if you want a smooth or rough finish or a painted or unpainted one.
- Keep your work space neat and clean.
- Work in a well-lit area.
- Use safety-related devices such as guards and hold-downs.

Exemplary Producers:

Gutzum Borglum	Timan Riemenschneider
Thomas Chippendale	William Rush
Samuel McIntire	Korczak Ziolkowski
William Morris	

Community Resources: Shop Teacher, Woodworker, Cabinet Maker

Quotes to Inspire:

"I saw the angel in the marble and carved until I set him free."

—Michelangelo

"Make visible what, without you, might perhaps never have been seen."

—Robert Bresson

Fishing Lure
by Dustin Gates

Dustin Gates is 14 years old and in the eighth grade at Weston High School in Weston, LA. He enjoys fine arts and literature and also plays basketball and throws javelin for his school. He has been interested in fishing since the age of four.

The assignment in our gifted class was to do a project. After brainstorming, I came up with the idea of researching about how fishing lures came to be. In my research, it was discovered that a lot of lures have been made using many different materials. Most of the first ones were made from balsa wood using any kind of knife available. As technology improved, whittler's knives that were specially made to carve wood were used. Experimentation with different types of wood was also undertaken. Cedar was a high-floating wood that was mainly used in the early 1920s. Cypress was a medium floater that was used in eastern Louisiana. Lures were made as realistic as possible during this era.

Experiments were later conducted with lures that had similar movements to those of a fish. During the decade of the '80s, plastic molds were used to make lures. In 1986, a bait called "Boy Howdy" constructed of plastic made its debut on the shelves in stores. One of my favorite plastic lures is the "Near Nuthin" plug made for fast twitching action. As new lures were introduced and their action was studied, it became apparent that wooden lures provided more similarity to the texture of the body of a fish. From this research, I got my idea to make a lure.

After sketching four different lures, I decided to model my lure after a "Louisiana Bug" made in the 1950s. Securing a piece of basswood and some whittler's knives, I began cutting and shaping my lure to give it the utmost action. Next, the lure was sanded and final details were made over the next few days. After finishing the body, the lure was painted in neutral colors. Textures were then added with iridescent colors, and fiery red eyes were created. Finally, hooks were added to the body.

The final evaluation was to test the lure to see if it worked. I went to my pier and on the first cast I caught a little tiny bass weighing about a pound. Even though it was a small fish, I was excited that my lure had worked as planned. While in the water, the lure descended down to the depth of about seven inches, just right for shallow water bass. My lure was a success; it moved perfectly.

My quote for others attempting new product ideas comes from Samuel Jackson: "Nothing will ever be attempted if all possible objectives must first be overcome."

Dustin's lure made from basswood based on his research.

Product Criteria Grid

Product: Carving

Components	Characteristics	Basic Materials
Title	• Appropriate to theme/topic, original	Assorted Materials Carving Tools Safety Equipment
Concept	• Relevant to topic and intended audience, unique	
Form	• Aesthetically appealing, proportionally correct, representative of concept	
Design	• Original, visually appealing, consideration of design principles and elements (i.e. balance, emphasis, variety, contrast, etc.)	
Texture	• Complementary to concept, enhancing	
Material/Medium	• Universal, significant to the events	

Product: Collage

Definition: A work of art composed of different materials assembled and pasted together in a unique fashion.

Title of the Expert: Artist

Types of Collage:

Abstract	Foil
Assemblage	Newspaper
Banner	Paper
Boxes	Stained Glass
Cloth	Steel/Metal
Construction	String
Decoupage	Wooden
Flag	

Words to Know:

Arranged	Found Objects
Banner	Glue
Cardboard	Paper
Combined	Paste
Cubism	Printed Materials
Dada	Realistic
Decoration	Scissors
Design	Soft Brush
Fabric	Texture
Flag	

Helpful Hints:

- Make pictures or objects that will excite, shock, and inform.
- You want the viewer to react to your work.
- Make collages that reflect societal problems/challenges: litter, water, pollution, etc.
- Look for materials everywhere you go: home, school, parks, etc.
- Use light to give a special effect.
- If you feel your work is not successful, try to determine how it can be improved.
- If your work turns out well, it is time to experiment and try new materials and ways of making collages.

Exemplary Producers:

Romare Bearden
Umberto Boccioni
George Braque
Eric Carle
John Chamberlain
Joseph Cornell
Arthur Dove
Max Ernst
Sue Fuller
Juan Gris
Ezra Jack Keats

Lio Lionni
Kasimir Malevich
Henri Matisse
Joan Miro
Louise Nevelson
Pablo Picasso
Robert Rauchenberg
Miriam Schapiro
Kurt Schwitters
Richard Stankiewicz
Vladimir Tatlin

Community Resources: Art Museum, Art Teacher, Graphic Artist

Quotes to Inspire:

"Every great work of art has two faces, one toward its own time and one toward the future, toward eternity."

—Daniel Barenboim

"All our knowledge has its origin in our perceptions."

—Leonardo da Vinci

Product Criteria Grid

Product: Collage

Components	Characteristics	Basic Materials
Title (optional)	• Relevant to theme, original	Construction Paper Fabric Scraps Found Objects Markers Old Magazines Paint Poster Board Rubber Cement Scissors
Theme	• Appropriate to topic and audience	
Materials	• Overlay of objects, connecting, planned in advance, appropriate areas emphasized, consideration of the elements and principles of design (i.e. balance, variety, movement, symmetry, emphasis, etc.), original, aesthetically appealing	
Color	• Related to theme, visually pleasing, enhancing, conveys appropriate mood/feeling	
Texture (optional)	• Appropriate for theme, complementary, aesthetically appealing	

Product: Costume

Definition: A piece of apparel, including accessories, depicting a certain culture, time period, profession, character, etc.

Title of the Expert: Costumier, Costume Designer

Types of Costumes:

Dramatic	Replica
Halloween	Stage
Historical	Theatrical
National	Traditional
Period	

Words to Know:

Accessory	Linen
Adornment	Mardi Gras
Alteration	Masks
Appliqué	Masquerade
Ascot	Millinery
Attire	Mini Skirt
Barbette	Motley
Basting	Mummer
Basque	Nap
Belt	Needle
Bias Tape	Net
Blazer	Organdy
Bobbin	Overcoat
Bodice	Palette
Bonnet	Palla
Bow tie	Panniers
Brim	Pattern
Brocade	Petticoat
Buckram	Pile
Bustle	Pinking Shears
Buttons	Piping
Calico	Piqué
Canvas	Plate
Cardigan	Pleats
Casing	Poncho
Chiffon	Presser Foot
Cloak	Rhinestones

Clogs	Ribbon
Collar	Robe
Color	Rosettes
Corset	Sari
Cotehardie	Sarong
Cotton	Sash
Corduroy	Satin
Cravat	Scallop
Crepe	Scarf
Crinoline	Scissors
Cuffs	Seam
Cutting Table	Seam Ripper
Dart	Sequin
Designer	Shawl
Drafting	Silk
Draping	Skirts
Dress Forms	Sleeve
Dress Rehearsal	Snaps
Embroider	Spangle
Ensemble	Stockings
Epaulets	Studded
Fabric	Suede
Face Putty	Taffeta
Fad	Tailcoat
Farthingale	Tape Measure
Felt	Taper
Finery	Tassel
Flapper	Texture
Frill	Thimble
Fringe	Tie
Frou Frou	Toga
Garment	Togs
Garter	Top Hat
Gather	Tracing Wheel
Gloves	Tricorn
Grommet	Trim
Hangers	Trinket
Headdresses	Trousers
Hem	Tunic
Hennin	Turban
Hook and Eye	Uniform
Hoop	Veils
Hose	VELCRO™
Houppelande	Velour

Jacket	Velvet
Jodhpurs	Vinyl
Kimono	Waist
Knickerbockers	Wardrobe
Knitting	Weaving
Lace	Wigs
Lame	Wool
Leather	Zipper
Line	

Helpful Hints:

- Design should be authentic to the period in time and enhance the script and production.
- Costumes must be durable enough to withstand the strain of performance.
- Read the script before developing the costume.
- A good thrift shop will have an unlimited supply of accessories.
- Measure each actor carefully.
- Costumes should be cleaned and pressed and kept in good repair during the run of the show.
- It is important to research the costumes and manners of the society the garment reflects.
- Books on historical costumes, paintings, fashion magazines, period pattern books, and social and cultural histories provide a general background for researching historical appropriateness.
- When selecting fabric, determine if the costume needs to be soft or stiff, lightweight or heavy, smooth or rough, shiny or matte. Also, consider how the fabric will react to light.
- Determine how the costume is to be utilized in movement prior to construction. For example, does it have to be changed quickly? Are pockets necessary? Much of this information should be found in the script.
- Fit the garment with the wrong side of the costume out for ease in alteration.
- When pinning the garment, place the pins with the points down.

Exemplary Producers:

Theoni Aldridge	Peter Seddon
Leon Nicholaevich Bakst	Bill Thomas
Sir Cecil Beaton	Diane Dalziel Vreeland
Marc Chagall	Tony Walton
Edith Head	Stanislaw Wyspianski
Pablo Picasso	Franco Zeffirelli
Ann Roth	Patricia Zipprott

Community Resources: Art Museum, Home Economics Teacher, Seamstress, Fabric Store, Professor of Theater, Historian

Quotes to Inspire:

"All costumes are caricatures. The basis of Art is not the Fancy Ball."

—Oscar Wilde

"Cost plays as important a consideration as design in costuming the cast."

—Beverly B. Ross and Jean P. Durgin

Fashion Throughout History

by Donna Moore

Donna Moore is an 18-year-old senior attending Heritage High School in Rockdale County, GA. She is an active member of Interact Club, National Honor Society, and Beta Club. She also participates in Symphonic Band and plays on the varsity softball team. Recently, she was named a University of Georgia Certificate of Merit Scholar. She was also accepted at the University of Georgia where she plans to major in Pre-Veterinary Medicine.

My world history teacher, Ms. McCullough, assigned the class a mastery project that involved developing creativity skills and improving research abilities. The theme was patterns throughout history and how they affect life today. We were given one month to research and complete the project. Ms. McCullough allowed us to work in groups as long as the finished product reflected the work completed by the group as a whole. Working with several of my close friends, Merrie Beth Lewis, Stephanie Boone, and Lisa Hamm, we decided that the only topic of interest to all of us was fashion. Once we had decided on the topic, gathering research material was not difficult. The library had several books that related to the topic. They contained a lot of information on clothing, accessories, and hairstyles. In addition, we also looked through fashion magazines to determine how styles today reflect those of the past.

While researching fashion, we discovered an excellent method for displaying our research. For years we have collected American Girl Dolls. There are five dolls in the collection, and each comes with a book that tells the stories of their lives. I still receive magazines in which I can order clothes and accessories for these dolls. Each doll represents a different period in American history, and among the four of us we had enough dolls to do a fashion show reflecting 11 different time periods. Our desire was to have the dolls represent history as authentically as possible.

Early Saturday morning we went to a nearby fabric store to select material for making dresses. We divided the dolls between us in order to find the cloth, lace, and trimming was needed in order to complete our individual dolls. We reviewed our notes and the cloth selected. Together we transformed our thoughts onto paper. We spent the rest of that day and every afternoon after school putting the costumes together piece by piece. Upon completion of the costumes, our notes were organized into the 11 time periods the dolls represented. Note cards were used to organize basic information on fashion of that time period and on events that may have influenced such fashions. Our research emphasized how fashion reflects the past and reoccurs throughout history.

Our project was presented for both of Ms. McCullough's classes, several librarians, and county office workers. In the process, we learned a lot about fashion; however, the best thing we learned is that it is possible to work hard and have fun doing it. The four of us got to know each other, learned to respect one another's opinions, and gained appreciation for the knowledge each brought to the project. Fashion may seem to involve only clothing, but it reflects many delicate signs and myths. For instance, in ancient Egypt, blue was the color that represented little boys, and was believed to protect them from evil. Little girls, on the other hand, were not worthy enough to be protected by such a strong color; and, later in history, girls were represented by the color pink. It signified that girls were made of everything sweet and good. Researching and presenting this project was extremely fun because we enjoyed learning about our selected topic. We suggest that others who are considering spending time and money on a project should choose one about which they will enjoy learning.

If students enjoy what they are doing, they are more likely to work diligently and produce better projects. Good research is also an important aspect of presenting a well-organized and thorough project. I believe that creating a product that inspires others to think and learn is one of the greatest abilities a person can have.

Pre-History

Greece & Rome

Mesopotamia

Egypt

Byzantium

Middle Ages

Renaissance

17th Century

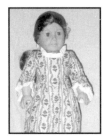
18th Century

19th Century

20th Century

Product Criteria Grid

Product: Costume

Components	Characteristics	Basic Materials
Style	• Appropriate to character, historically accurate, properly fitted	Fabric Needle Pattern Scissors Sewing Machine Straight Pins Tape Measure Thread
Material/Fabric	• Durable, appropriate to season depicted, historically accurate	
Color	• Appropriate to character and intended mood, consideration of light effects	
Accessories (optional)	• Enhance costume, appropriate to character, historically accurate, realistic	

Product: Diorama

Definition: A scene constructed in three dimensions.

Title of Expert: Modeler

Types of Dioramas:

Historical	Scientific
Habitat	Story
Military	

Words to Know:

Accessories	Magnifying Lens
Airbrush	Miniature
Assembly	Plan
Authentic	Presentation
Balance	Putty
Balsa Wood	Replica
Base	Resin
Blending	Scale
Dead Space	Scene
Decal	Scratchbuilding
Design	Scribing Lines
Detailing	Shading
Display	Shadows
Distance	Sprue
Dry Brushing	Terrain
Figure	Washes
Landscaping	Weathering
Layout	Work Space
Lighting	

Helpful Hints:

- Use parts of commercially prepared kits when necessary.
- Strive for authenticity.
- Select a major focus of attention.
- Keep all pieces together in a plastic bag.
- Put pieces together without gluing first to make sure they align properly.
- Paint small and hard-to-reach pieces prior to assembling.
- Always apply light colors before darker ones when painting.
- Follow directions carefully.

- Choose a work area that is well-lit.
- Keep work surface clean and organized.
- Keep a supply of clean rags on hand for spills.
- Decals must be handled with the utmost care, as they are usually very fragile.
- Use appropriate glue for your surfaces. The wrong glue can be a disaster.
- Save your scraps! You can use them on your next model.

Exemplary Producers:

Ray Anderson	Louis Jacques Mandé Daguerre
Dr. Harold Auerhan	Shepard Paine
C. M. Bouton	Ron Volstad
Ron Clark	

Community Resources: Art Teacher, Hobby Store, Modelers

Quotes to Inspire:

"Although dioramas have long been an accepted form of display for museums, their popularity as a hobby is a relatively recent development."

—Shepard Paine

"Nature is inside art as its content, not outside as its model."

—Northrop Frye

Product Criteria Grid

Product: Diorama

Components	Characteristics	Basic Materials
Title (optional)	• Relevant to subject/topic, prominent, legible, correct spelling and grammar	Cardboard Box Construction Paper Fabric Found Objects Glue Index Cards Markers Miniature figures Scissors Wood Scraps
Casing	• Stable, proper size, appropriate material, positioned for viewing, resists tampering	
Background	• Neat, natural to the event or entity, accurate scale, complementary of other components	
Objects	• Well-constructed, appropriate for event or theme, proportional, detailed, realistic, suitably placed	
Place Card	• Appropriately titled, clear, concise, easy to read, proper spelling, prominently placed	
Lighting (optional)	• Unobtrusive, precisely directed, safe, enhancing, reliable	

Product: Graph

Definition: A visual representation of numerical data that facilitates the presentation of two or more facts for comparative purposes in order to reinforce comprehension.

Title of the Expert: Mathematician, Statistician

Types of Graphs:

Bar
Circular
Column
Cosmograph
Cross-Hatched
Diagram
Flow
Gannt Chart
Grid
Histogram
Layer
Line
Logarithmic

Nomograph
Organizational
Pictograph
Pie
Scale
Scatter
Shaded
Solid
Tabular
Trilinear
Venn Diagram
Webbing

Words to Know:

Alignment
Axis
Bell Curve
Cartesian
Categorical
Center
Circle
Column
Continuous
Coordinate
Criterion Variable
Data
Dependent Variable
Discrete
Distribution
Equality
Equation
Fixed
Frequency

Legend
Line
Line-of-Best-Fit
Locus
Number Pairs
Origin
Pairs
Plan
Plot
Point
Predictor Variable
Proportion
Quadrant
Relationship
Scale
Set
Subset
Statistics
Tabulation

Geometry	Theory
Horizontal	Trend
Independent Variable	Trigonometry
Inequality	Variables
Intersection	Vector
Interval	Vertical
Key	

Helpful Hints:

- Use graph paper to help in the planning process.
- Make use of rulers, compasses, protractors, etc.
- The independent variable is almost always recorded on the horizontal axis and the dependent variable on the vertical axis.
- The title should clearly communicate the purpose of the graph.
- The value of the horizontal axis is written first, followed by the value of the vertical axis. The two numbers are separated with a comma and are placed in parentheses, for example (2,8).
- To determine scale, find the difference between the largest values for the variable. Divide the difference by five for a reasonable number of intervals.
- Too many intervals crowd a graph and make it difficult to plot points.
- Select the type of graph appropriate to display your data. If data are continuous, a line graph may be best. If intervals between data have no meaning, a bar graph may be appropriate.

Exemplary Producers:

Jacques Bertin	Ross Perot
René Descartes	William Playfair
John B. Peddle	

Community Resources: Math Teacher/Professor, Graphic Artist, Statistician

Quotes to Inspire:

" ... with the assistance of these charts, such information will be got,
without the fatigue and trouble of studying the particulars of which it is composed."
—William Playfair

"It is a capital mistake to theorize before one has data."
—Sir Anthony Conan Doyle

"Data is what distinguishes the dilettante from the artist."
—George V. Higgins

Product Criteria Grid

Product: Graph

Components	Characteristics	Basic Materials
Title	• Legible, neat, correct spelling, prominent, relates to data	Calculator Compass Computer Graph Paper Paper Pencil Protractor Ruler
Style	• Appropriate for data type, easy to interpret, orderly, non-cluttered	
Data	• Accurate, relevant to title	
Labels/Key	• Legible, neat, correctly placed to correspond with data	

Product: Map

Definition: A graphic representation of the Earth or other celestial bodies' surface or atmosphere.

Title of Expert: Mapmaker, Cartographer, Surveyor, Topographer, Geographic Information System Specialist

Types of Maps:

Aerial	Interactive
Atlas	Isoline
Block-Diagram	Isometric
Cadastral	Isopleths
Cartogram	Land
Chart	Navigation
Choropleth	Photomap
Classification	Pin
Climatic	Planimetric
Computer-Generated	Plat
Contour	Prism
Dasymetric	Propaganda
Demographic	Relief
Dot-Type	Representational
Flood-Plain	Road
Flow-line	Seismicity
Geographic	Subject
Geologic	Thematic
Hatch	Topographic
Hydrography	Weather

Words to Know:

Alidale	Landsat
Atlas	Latitude
Axis	Legend
Census	Longitude
Color	Meridian
Compass	Parallel
Contour	Perspective
Coordinates	Photogrammetry
Datum	Plot
Digital Evaluation Model	Plotter
Digital Line Graph	Population
Digitizer	Prime Meridian

Direction
Distance
Drafting Tape
Elevation
Equator
Formation
Geodesy
Geographic Info System
Global Positioning
Globe
Graphics
Great Circle
Hachure
Hypsography
Irregular Curve
Isallobar
Isobar
Isogram
Isohel
Isohyet
Isotherm
Key

Projection
Protractor
Public Land Survey
Raster
Remote Sensing
Rhumb Line
Rulers
Satellite
Scale
Shading
Speleology
Statistics
Survey
Symbol
T-Square
Template
Terrain
Triangles
Trimetrogon
Universal Transverse Mercator
Vector
Vegetation

Helpful Hints:

- You should be familiar with the basic equipment used to make a map (i.e. compass, templates, rulers, triangles, T-square, computer, plotter, printer, etc.) and how to use them properly and with online map resources.
- Lines and text should be sharp, crisp, and easy to read.
- Work with clean hands on a clean surface to avoid smudging.
- Lay out drawings in pencil first, and then prepare your final draft in ink.
- Remember, accuracy is essential in mapmaking.
- Familiarize yourself with certain colors and symbols that have been established as standard representations on maps.
- Select the map type and projection that best represents the data and purpose you have.

Exemplary Producers:

al-Idrisi
al-Khwerizmi
Benjamin Banneker
Martin Behalm
Barbara Buttenfield
Sebastian Cabot

Henricus Hondius
Alexis Jaillot
Eusebio Francisco Kino
Johann Lambert
Johann Tobias Mayer
Gerhardus Mercator

The Cassini Family
William Clark
Jack Dangermond
William Morris Davis
Eratosthenes of Cyrene
Howard Fisher
John Charles Fremont
Henry Gannett
Edmund Halley
Henry Harness
Chang Heng
Sven Anders von Hedin
Augustine Hermann
Hipparchus

Andrew McNally
John Mitchell
Abraham Ortelius
Donna Pequet
Claudius Ptolemy
William H. Rand
Nicholas Sanson
William Scoresby
John Smow
John Smith Strabo
Roger Tomlinson
David Thompson
John White
Pei Xu

Community Resources: Professor of Geography, Surveyor, United States Geological Survey

Quotes to Inspire:

"The world can doubtless never be well known by theory: practice is absolutely necessary; but surely it is of great use to a young man, before he sets out for that country, full of mazes, windings, and turnings, to have at least a general map of it, made by some experienced traveler."
—Lord Chesterfield

"I have an existential map; it has 'you are here' written all over it."
—Steven Wright

"We shall not cease from exploration
And the end of all our exploring
will be to arrive where we started
And know the place for the first time."
—T. S. Eliot

"A map is anything that shows you the way from one point to another, from one level of understanding to another. A map depicts the route through information, be it a geographic locale or a philosophic treatise."
—Richard Saul Wurman

Product Criteria Grid

Product: Map

Components	Characteristics	Basic Materials
Title	• Large, neat, legible, accurate, corresponds with theme	Atlas Compass Computer
Key/Legend	• Appropriately coded, concise, neat, legible, simple	Erasers Globe India Ink
Direction	• Accurate, appropriately placed within view	Markers Paints Paper
Scale	• Accurate, appropriate to map size	Pencils Protractor
Grid (optional)	• Neat, consistent/uniform	Rulers Stencils
Graphics (optional)	• Visually appealing, neat, appropriate to map and theme	T-Squares Templates Triangles

Product: Mobile

Definition: A sculpture consisting of carefully balanced parts that move.

Title of the Expert: Sculptor/Sculptress

Types of Mobiles:

Abstract	Screw
Mechanical	Self-supporting
Paper	Spiral
Pinwheel	Swaying
Rocking	Topic

Words to Know:

Abstract	Kinetic
Air	Manipulation
Arms	Movement
Assembly	Pivot
Balance	Shapes
Base	Suspension
Equilibrium	Thread
Gravity	Vertical
Horizontal	Wire

Helpful Hints:

- If you are a beginner, choose materials that are easy to manipulate.
- Make use of color to add extra interest and effect.
- For bending wire, a pair of round-nosed pliers is ideal.
- Be creative with your materials and design.
- Remember, mobiles do not have to hang down from the ceiling; they can also stick up from the ground or out from a wall as long as they move.
- Do not tie strings too tightly for you may have to move them to achieve balance.
- Experiment until you find each point of balance.
- Experiment with different weights of materials.
- A drill may be necessary to make holes in collected objects for hanging.

Exemplary Producers:

Pol Bury	George Rickey
Alexander Calder	Aleksandr Rodchenko
Kenneth Martin	Takumi Shinagawa

Community Resources: Sculptor, Art Teacher, Art Museum Curator, Art Critic

Quotes to Inspire:

"A work of art is above all an adventure of the mind."

—Eugene Ionesco

"Art is idea. It is not enough to draw, paint, and sculpt. An artist should be able to think."

—Gordon Woods

Product Criteria Grid

Product: Mobile

Components	Characteristics	Basic Materials
Title (optional)	• Prominent, relevant to theme, viewable	Construction Paper Drill Found Objects Glue Hole Punch Scissors String Wire
Construction/Design	• Interesting, complex, stable	
Parts	• Sturdy, secure, invisible, relevant to theme, engaging, viewable, aesthetically appealing	
Movement	• Motion present	
Balance	• Adjusted to produce desired effect	

Product: Mural

Definition: A picture painted directly on a wall, ceiling, floor, or similar surface.

Title of Expert: Muralist

Types of Murals:

Commemorative	Photographic
Fresco	Scenic
Historical	Tape
Landscape	Tiled

Words to Know:

Airbrush	Layout
Background	Light
Burner	Small Format
Color	Scale
Composition	Sketch
Concept	Stereochromy
Exhibition	Techniques
Extended Format	Value
Foreground	

Helpful Hints:

- If the mural will be displayed outdoors, select a paint that will withstand the weather.
- Sketch on paper first to determine proper proportions.
- Select images that will enhance the surrounding environment.
- Check accuracy of details before painting.
- Make creative use of available space.
- Obtain necessary permissions and permits.
- Select colors that will compliment the surrounding environment and enhance the details of the mural.

Exemplary Producers:

Judy Baca	José Clemente Orozco
Thomas Hart Benton	Maxfield Frederick Parrish
Mary Cassatt	Pablo Picasso
Marc Chagall	Pierre Puvis de Chavannes
Stuart Davis	Diego Rivera
Hippolyte Paul Delaroche	Peter Paul Rubens

John La Farge	John Singer Sargent
Gwyn Jones	Ben Shahn
Reginald Marsh	Everett Shinn
Gari Melchers	David Alfaro siqueiros

Community Resource People: Art Teacher, Local Artist, Muralist

Quotes to Inspire:

"There is nothing more difficult for a truly creative painter than to paint a rose, because before he can do so he has first to forget all the roses that were ever painted."

—Henri Matisse

"Every artist dips his brush in his own soul, and paints his own nature into his pictures."

—Henry Ward Beecher

Product Criteria Grid

Product: Mural

Components	Characteristics	Basic Materials
Title	• Relevant to theme/concept, original, thought-provoking	Drop Cloth Measuring Tape Paint Paint Brushes Paper Pencil Stencils
Concept	• Relevant to topic, significant to intended audience, appeals to a wide audience	
Color	• Visually appealing, appropriate to images and/or concept	
Design/Layout	Interesting, well-planned, consideration of design, principle elements, (i.e., balance, emphasis, variety, contrast, etc.)	
Images	• Clear, relevant to topic/concept, appropriate for intended audience, proportional	
Text (optional)	• Neat, correct spelling and grammar, contrasts with background for ease in reading, corresponds with images and concept, clearly presents intended message	

Product: Photograph

Definition: An image printed by means of light and chemicals onto a piece of paper.

Title of the Expert: Photographer

Types of Photography:

Abstract	Micro
Aerial	Montage
Close-Up	Motion Picture
Documentary	Nature
Fashion	Panoramic
Formalistic	Photojournalism
Free Lance	Polaroid
Glamour	Portrait
Industrial	Scientific
Journalism	Special Effects
Landscape	Sports/Action
Macro	Still Life

Words to Know:

Activator	Luminance
Airbrush	Matting
Angle	Monopods
Aperture	Negative
Astro	Panorama
Backlighting	Paper
Balance	Perspective
Battery	Preservative
Bleaching	Print
Camera	Print Tongs
Chromogenic	Processor
Composition	Reducer
Contact Sheet	Refraction
Contrast	Reportage
Cropping	Restrainer
Developer	Saturation
Diffusion	Solvent
Distortion	Stabilizer
Dodging	Shadow
Drying	Shutter
Emulsion	Slide

Enlargement	Speed
Exposure	Telephoto Lens
Film	Tripod
Filter	Wide-Angle Lens
Fixer	Stop Bath
Flash	Timer
Focus	Tonality
Frame	Tone
Hue	Trays
Hypo Eliminator	Trimmer
Image	Vignetting
Lens	Wash
Light	Wetting Agent
Light Meter	Zoom Lens

Helpful Hints:

- Select an appropriate camera.
- Choose film according to desired outcome.
- Look at your subject from different angles.
- Keep a scrapbook of interesting photographs to use as references.
- If you have limited funds, consider buying a used camera.
- Review books on photography for techniques.
- Attend photographic exhibits.
- Take lots of photographs so you have a wide array from which to choose.
- Keep your equipment clean. Lenses must be free from dirt, dust, and fingerprints.
- Study the work of several photographers whose work you admire.
- Experiment with different shutter speeds and flash illumination.
- Protect film from heat and humidity, and note the expiration date on film.
- Think of careers where you may employ the use of photography.

Exemplary Producers:

Berenice Abbott	William Henry Jackson
Ansel Adams	Yousaf Karsh
Edie Adams	Andre Kertesz
Diane Arbus	Edwin Land
Eve Arnold	Dorothea Lange
Eugene Atget	Russel Lee
Richard Avedon	Jules Lion
David Bailey	Mary Ellen Mark
James Ball	Nicholas Nixon
Cornelius Battey	Timothy O'Sullivan
Jessie Tarbox Beals	Gorden Parks

Margaret Bourke-White   Irving Penn
Mathew Brady   Eliot Porter
Bill Brandt   Man Ray
Julia Margaret Cameron   Jacob Riis
Robert Capa   Herb Ritz
Henri Cartier-Bresson   Sandy Scoglund
Joe Costa   Addison Scurlock
Gerry Craham   Cindy Sherman
Imogene Cunningham   Lorna Simpson
Louis Degueer   W. Eugene Smith
Alfred Eisenstadt   Edward Steichen
Walker Evans   Gertrude Stein
Roger Fenton   Alfred Stieglitz
Robert Frank   Paul Strand
Lee Friedlander   Henry Fox Talbot
Flor Garduno   Peter Turner
Rolph Gobits   Jerry Uelsmann
Ernst Haas   Augustus Washington
Frank Herrman   Thomas Wedgewood
Louis W. Hine   Edward Weston
Tana Hoban   Minor White

Community Resources: Art Teacher, Camera Stores, Photographer, Photographic Contests and Exhibitions

Quotes to Inspire:

"The camera is an instrument that teaches people how to see without a camera."
—Dorothea Lange

"A photograph is a secret about a secret. The more it tells you the less you know."
—Diane Arbus

"I paint what cannot be photographed, that which comes from the imagination or from dreams, or from an unconscious drive. I photograph the things that I do not wish to paint, the things which already have an existence."
—Man Ray

Product Criteria Grid

Product: Photograph

Components	Characteristics	Basic Materials
Title (optional)	• Relevant to topic/concept, original	Camera Developer Film Matting (optional) Props (if necessary) Tripod
Subject/Setting	• Appropriate for the theme/topic, visually interesting	
Focus	• Sharp, clear	
Light	• High quality, varied to create desired effect	
Angle	• Skillfully selected, presents unique perspective	
Composition	• Interesting choice and arrangement, consideration of foreground and background, appropriate emphasis	

Product: Poster

Definition: A relatively large printed and decorative card, paper, or placard for posting.

Title of the Expert: Graphic Designer, Lithographer, Artist

Types of Posters:

Advertisement	Lithograph
Announcement	Patriotic
Business	Political
Commercial	Photographic
Decorative	Promotional
Event	Propaganda
Informative	Social Issues
Illustration	Theatrical

Words to Know:

Airbrush	Layout
Balance	Lithograph
Bleed	Logo
Boldface	Margin
Border	Matte
Calligraphy	Medium
Caricature	Mounting
Clip Art	Overlay
Composition	Plates
Concept	Proportion
Contrast	Readability
Cropping	Serif/Sans Serif
Embossing	Type
Font	Slogan
Function	Standard Sizes
Glossy	Tracing
Graphic Design	Trim
Graphics	Typeface
Headings	Stencil
Illustration	Style

Helpful Hints:

- Use stencils for lettering.
- Sketch poster on scratch paper before determining final design.

- Study posters around town. Decide which are most successful.
- Colors should be contrasting for easy reading, both in color and value.
- Simplicity should be kept in mind.
- Your poster should have a clear statement of purpose.
- The title should be short and attention-grabbing.
- The title should be readable at a distance of four feet.
- The title's typeface should be bold and about 30 mm high.
- Transfer letters are an excellent alternative for lettering.
- White space is important. Avoid clutter.
- Make it clear what is to be looked at first, second, and so forth.
- Handouts may be prepared with more detailed information.
- All kinds of photos, graphs, drawings, cartoons, paintings, and so forth can be used.
- Go to the library and look at books on posters.
- Study current graphic design journals.

Exemplary Producers:

Oskar Saul Bass	Gustav Klimt
Aubrey Beardsley	Henri de Toulouse-Lautrec
Beggarstaff Brothers	Alfred Leete
Pierre Bonnard	El Lissitzky
Will Bradley	E'douard Manet
A. M. Cassandre	Peter Max
Jules Cheret	Victor Moscoso
Paul Colin	Kolo Moser
Nathanial Currier	Alphonse Mucha
Kokoschka Daumier	Maxfield Parrish
Max Ernst	Edward Penfield
M. C. Escher	Pablo Picasso
George de Feure	Ethel Reed
Otto Fischer	Norman Rockwell
James Flagg	Egon Schiele
Paul Gavarni	Ben Shahn
Charles Dana Gibson	Saul Steinberg
Milton Glaser	M. Louise Stowell
Eugene Grasset	Tomi Ungerer
James Merrit Ives	Andy Warhol
E. McKnight Kauffer	Adolphe Willette

Community Resources: Graphic Artist, Art Teacher, Copying/Printing Center, Marketing Consultant

Quotes to Inspire:

"Advertising is the greatest art form of the twentieth century."

—Marshall McLuhan

"Every child is an artist. The problem is how to remain an artist once he grows up."

—Pablo Picasso

Product Criteria Grid

Product: Poster

Components	Characteristics	Basic Materials
Title	• Legible, neat, correct spelling, prominent, large enough to be read at a distance, representative of the poster theme	Construction Paper Markers Paint Paper Pen Pencils Poster Paper Rubber Cement Rulers Scissors Stencils Transfer Letters
Labels	• Legible, neat, appropriately placed to correspond with graphics (if present), use of appropriate grammar and spelling	
Graphics	• Clearly visible, appropriate for poster theme, neatly displayed, securely attached to poster backing, matted (optional), visually appealing	
Layout	• Balance, non-cluttered, prominent graphics and/or text, interesting, flowing from area of most emphasis to area of least emphasis	

Product: Quilt

Definition: A decorative stitching usually made of fabric.

Title of Expert: Quilter

Types of Quilts:

Album	Medley
Appliqué	Patchwork
Biscuit	Picture
Brides	Pieced
Crazy	Presentation
Friendship	Scrap
Lap	Story
Marriage	Tied
Medallion	Trapunto

Words to Know:

All-Quilted	Frame
All-White	French Knot
Amish	Heirloom
Appliqué	Hem
Back Stitch	Motley
Backing	Needlework
Balance	Overlap
Batting	Pique
Binding	Running Stitch
Blanket Stitch	Satin Stitch
Block	Seeding Stitch
Cross Stitch	Stitch
Duvet	Template
Edging	Textile
Embroidery	Thimble
Fabric	Trapunto
Fern Stitch	Trim
Filler	Tufting
Flat Quilting	Wadded Quilting

Helpful Hints:

- Plan your quilt on paper first.
- Measure accurately. Using two yardsticks is suggested for larger pieces.

- If it doesn't turn out as you pictured—try again.
- Do not make the same item twice. Try something new!
- Do not demand perfection.
- Pre-wash fabrics before beginning.
- Write your ideas down on paper so you will not forget them.
- Don't sit too long. Exercise and stretch frequently.
- Work in a well-lit area to avoid strain on your eyes.
- Remember, all ages and both genders can quilt.
- Always fold your quilts right side in and air them often.
- Be creative with color and design.
- Record the history or process of the quilt and store it along with the quilt.
- Never give away your first quilt. Keep it for your family.
- Do not tackle too large of a project; yet, do not undertake one too small and lacking challenge.
- Consider entering quilting competitions. You will learn a lot from examining other quilter's work.

Exemplary Producers:

Lenice Ingram Bacon	Carrie Hall
Mary Barton	Marguerite Ickis
Jinny Beyer	Michael James
Hazel Carter	Florence Peto
Averil Colby	Yvonne Porcella
Nancy Crow	Grace Snyder
Amy Emms	Bertha Stenge
Jeffrey Gutcheon	Marie Webster

Community Resources: Fabric Store, Seamstress, Quilting Bee/Guild, Quilting Exhibits/Competitions, Parents/Grandparents

Quotes to Inspire:

"A line will take us hours maybe;
Yet if it does not seem a moment's thought,
Our stitching and unstitching has been naught."

—W. B. Yeats

"The best way to have a good idea is to have lots of ideas."

—Linus Pauling

"Use what talent you possess: The woods would be very silent
if no birds sang except those that sang best."

—Henry Van Dyke

Story Quilt

by Krystle Nicole Cash

Krystle Nicole Cash is 13 years old and lives in Chatham, LA. She is in the eighth grade at Chatham High School where she plays junior varsity basketball and is an active member of the Character Counts Program and the Beta Club. In her spare time, she enjoys writing and creating new ideas. She believes that starting something new is like beginning a new horizon, never ending, but going on and on until you look up and see your creation and admire it because it is a new road to your imagination.

My research was on Faith Ringgold, an African American female artist. Her style of art is mainly based on story quilts of all types. The research on her gave me inspiration to design my own story quilt out of papers, paints, glue, and ribbons. These materials were used due to the time limit for the project.

This project included writing a fictional story to be put on the quilt. I wrote, "Be Careful What You Wish For (You Might Just Get It)," which is about a young girl my age, named Nicole. She moved with her family from the warm climate of Louisiana to North Dakota. She despised the cold weather, and one night wished upon a star for hot weather. The weather did not change immediately, so like an impatient child she became discouraged and told herself it was silly to wish on a mere shooting star. Soon she became aware of a warming trend happening, and because the heat became extreme, lots of people got sick, including her little sister. Everyone blamed El Niño, but deep in her heart Nicole knew that it was because of her wish. So when she saw another shooting star, she wished for normal weather, and the next day it snowed. In the end, she reminds us that you should be careful what you wish for because you might get it!

This project incorporated uses of language arts skills and techniques, art and media, and problem solving. While doing this project, progress was evaluated frequently by checking to see if the materials selected were appropriate to achieve the results I wanted. For example, was the glue holding? Is the writing accurate? As I constructed the quilt, my gifted and talented teacher and I had oral critiques on how it was progressing, such as the use of color scheme, balance, and other design elements. While creating this project, I focused on and learned more about the art of writing, too.

I shared this project with my gifted and talented teacher, schoolmates, other teachers, parents, siblings, and relatives. The story quilt was also put on display at the Jackson Parish Library.

Art is a great skill. Some people say you have to set steps and follow them all the way through completion. I say any mix-up that may happen while creating your project leads to another road to your imagination.

To enhance your learning abilities, creating your own ideas is very important. I liked the fact that my research showed in my project. To any one else who would like to go that extra mile with creativity, go ahead! There is nothing wrong with doing something new, especially when the new idea comes from you. My favorite quote to share with others is one by Verne Hill: "If you always do what you always did you will always get what you always got."

This is a quilt created by Krystle depicting a scene from her fictional story.

Product Criteria Grid

Product: Quilt

Components	Characteristics	Basic Materials
Title (optional)	• Relevant to topic/concept, original	Adornments (optional) Needle Paper Patterns Pencil Scissors Sewing Machine Templates Thimble Thread
Concept	• Relevant to topic	
Planning	• Well-organized, layout/design made in advance, systematic	
Fabric	• Durable, suitable for quilt purposes	
Panels	• Large enough to complete design, appropriate color scheme and variation, consistent	
Stitching	• Even, neat, blends with background or stands out for attention	
Design/Layout	• Original, interesting, visually appealing, pre-planned, consideration of design principles and elements (i.e. balance, emphasis, variety, contrast)	
Color	• Enhances design, corresponds to topic/theme, aesthetically appealing	

Product: Sculpture

Definition: A three-dimensional work of art.

Title of the Expert: Sculptor/Sculptress

Types of Sculptures:

Bronze
Carved
Clay
Copper
Engraving
Found Objects
Glass
Glyptic
Gold
Granite
Greenware
Intaglio
Kinetic
Marble
Metal

Outdoor
Papier Mache
Plaster
Plastic
Porcelain
Relief
Silver
Soap
Stone
Terra Cotta
Water
Wax
Wire
Wood

Words to Know:

Abstract
Akrolith
Angular
Annealing
Armature
Bisque
Boucharde
Bust
Carving
Casing
Cast
Chisel
Commission
Contour
Elongated
Fire

Form
Geometric
Glaze
Kiln
Mallets
Modular
Plane
Plaster
Realistic
Relief
Scoring
Shape
Technique
Texture
Vibrating

Helpful Hints:

- Relate a message through sculpture.
- Be sure your sculpture is sturdy.
- Experiment with different materials.
- Consider both vertical and horizontal space.
- If your sculpture is to be displayed outside, select a material that will withstand the elements of weather.
- Find spaces indoors and outdoors that can be enhanced with sculpture.

Exemplary Producers:

Alexander Archipenko
Jean Arp
Ernst Barlack
George Grey Barnard
Mary Bauermeister
Giovanni Bologna
Gutzon Borglum
Emile Antoine Bourdelle
Constantin Brancusi
Henri Gaudier-Brzeska
Alexander Calder
Benvenuto Cellini
José Benito Churriguera
Thomas Crawford
Jo Davidson
Edgar Degas
Donatello
Sir Jacob Epstein
John Flaxman
Daniel Chester French
Horatio Gennough
Alberto Giacometti
Dame Barbara Hepworth
Malvina Hoffman
Allan Houser
Donald Judd
Wilhelm Lehmbruck
Jacque Lipchitz
Richard Lippold
Lysippos
Paul Manship

Artiside Maillol
Henry Matisse
Michaelangelo
Michelozzi Michelozzo
Henry Moore
Myron
Louise Nevelson
Isamu Noguchi
Nicola Pisano
Polydorus
Polykleitos
Mary Ray
Frederick Remington
Pierre Auguste Renoir
William Rimmer
Faith Ringgold
Auguste Rodin
John Rogers
Theodore Roszak
William Rush
Lucas Samaras
Andreas Schluter
Nicholas Schoffer Scopas
George Segal
David Smith
Tony Smith
Andrea del Verrochio
George Frederick Watts
Robert Wilson
Patience Lovell Wright
Kriczak Ziolkowski

Community Resources: Art Teacher, Museum Director, Sculptor

Quotes to Inspire:

"The marble not yet carved can hold the form
of every thought the greatest artist has."

—Michelangelo

"What sculpture is to a block of marble,
education is to a human soul."

—Joseph Addison

"Sculpture is the art of intelligence."

—Pablo Picasso

"There are three forms of visual art: Painting is art to look at,
sculpture is art you can walk around,
and architecture is art you can walk through."

—Dan Rice

Electricity City:
A Time Line of Charleston Architecture

by (front l to r) Alison Filosa, Cameron Smith, Kaity Allen, Thomas Disher, Blake Kaplan, Justin Mitchell, Samantha Ingram; (back) Christopher Brooks, Cantey Bissell, Brian Holmes, Thomas Willi, Edward Buckley, Brittany Barrett, Cole Lawrimore, Kyle Bates, Katherine Hildebrandt, Erynn Carroll, Mary Gene Smith, Melissa Floyd, and Michelle Carl

This group of fourth-grade students who constructed these buildings attended James B. Edwards Elementary School in Mt. Pleasant, SC. They are enrolled in Charleston County's gifted and talented program entitled Students Actively Involved in Learning (SAIL). They are currently students at Moultrie Middle School in Mt. Pleasant.

Mt. Pleasant is just across the river from Charleston, which is a historic city full of 18th-century buildings. This project was selected by our teacher, Jenny Hane, and was a problem-based learning unit called "Electricity City," developed by The College of William and Mary. It was related to our current topic of study "Needs of the City."

The project was initiated by going to downtown Charleston to tour the historic district with Mr. Bill Smyth, who is the coordinator of social studies for Charleston County Schools. He was very helpful and taught us a lot about different types of architecture. Our buildings were selected by choosing the styles of architecture that appealed to us and would be the most fun to build. Some of them were public buildings and some were privately owned.

We learned about the features of each style of architecture, from early Colonial with its dormers, paneled shutters, and gabled roofs, to Georgian with its boxy symmetry and central halls. In addition, the Federal Period with its fanlights, rounded windows, and balustrades was explored along with the Classic Revival with its columns and pediments. The Victorian Period with its turrets and elaborate woodwork was also examined.

Before our products could be developed, each building was researched thoroughly. Charleston tour guides and newspaper articles about each building that had been renovated were used to gather information. Previous owners and employees of the buildings were also interviewed. Accurate measurements of each building were made using a tape measure to measure the length, width, and distance between the windows and doors. Side elevation drawings were made on clipboards. In addition, a five-foot pole marked with black tape at every foot was used in each photograph to indicate the overall height of the building. When the pictures were developed, this pole provided a visual scale in each picture, thus assisting us in determining the actual height of each.

Before constructing the buildings, foam board and nine-volt batteries were purchased. Foam board was selected because it is light, but sturdy, and comes in different colors. It also has two sides in case of error. Using the previously gathered measurements, we began drawing the walls of the buildings on the foam board. It is important to measure in from the straight edge in two places in order to draw a straight line. The outside walls were cut with a large utility knife using a ruler for a straight edge. Leather gloves were worn for protection. Reference was made back to the photographs to verify measurements. A ruler was used to measure for windows and doors. A paper pattern could also be used for this purpose. After the windows and doors were drawn on the foam board walls, a ruler and small exacto knife were used to cut them out. Windows were made of overhead transparency strips, and fine white paint pens were used to draw the panes. The roof and shutters were constructed with mat board scraps.

Special features, such as bay windows and columns were recreated to achieve full detail in the buildings. Many of these architectural elements were designed through experimentation. A tile roof was made by peeling the outside layer of a cardboard box, and columns were constructed by scoring on foam board and forming a curved edge. Wooden dowels were also used for columns. The shingles were recreated by taking mat board strips, cutting them into little squares, and gluing them to the roof in an overlapping fashion. Additionally, turrets were built by peeling cardboard and forming it into cones. These features made our buildings come alive.

We learned many important things during this project. For example, we learned to always paint both sides of the foam board. The reason for this is that painting only one side results in warping or bending. By painting windows with a fine white paint pen or an extra fine permanent pen, they look better and are more realistic. Strips of transparencies should be used for windows, and the panes should be drawn before the building is glued together.

Once the buildings were completed, it was time to give them lights. A series circuit would not produce a bright enough light, so a parent suggested learning about a parallel circuit using 12 lights. After cutting 12 lights from the strand, wire strippers were used at both ends. To avoid burning out the light, each was checked for just a second on the battery to see if it worked properly. We put the lights together by twisting the wires very tightly to make good connections, and tested them by trying to pull them apart. An adult soldered the connections, and electric tape was used to hang the lights in the buildings. The switches and batteries were then attached.

This was a very long project, but one we all liked. Some of us especially liked the building part and getting to work with adult tools, thus proving we could be careful and responsible. Others enjoyed the math and problem solving involved with making special architectural features. Everyone loved the electricity, and we learned a lot about history and architecture, including accurate measurement, building a model to scale, and adding details to make models come alive.

We also learned how to write about buildings and present history in an interesting way to others. The Time Line of Architecture was shared with fourth-grade classes and at PTA meetings. Teachers at a meeting of the South Carolina Consortium for Educators of Gifted Students loved our work and asked many questions about how they could also attempt this project with their students. Our advice to anyone who tries this is to measure accurately, cut carefully, and take the time to get the details right.

Alison Filosa stands with the five foot pole that allowed the students to figure the height of the building in front of the Pink House. It is thought to be the oldest house in Charleston, SC.

Erynn Carroll and Mary Gene Smith make electrical circuits out of Christmas tree lights to illuminate their Colonial houses.

(front l to r) Justin Mitchell with Georgian house on corner of Tradd and Meeting Streets, Cameron Smith with Pink House from Colonial period; (back) Samantha Ingram with Old Exchange from the Georgian period, Thomas Disher with City Hall from Federal style, and Katherine Hildebrandt with the Old Exchange.

Product Criteria Grid

Product: Sculpture

Components	Characteristics	Basic Materials
Concept	• Relevant to topic and intended audience, accurate	Assorted Materials Clay Plaster Sculpting Tools Water Wire
Base	• Sturdy, proportional to sculpture, non-distracting	
Form	• Aesthetically appealing, proportionally correct, representative of subject/concept	
Design	• Original, visually appealing, consideration of design principles and elements (i.e. balance, emphasis, variety, contrast, etc.)	
Texture	• Complementary to concept, enhancing	
Medium/Material	• Durable, appropriate for design, suitable for display environment	

Visual Resources
Cartoon

Books

Bulloch, I., & Hynes, S. (1998). *Cartoons and animation.* Chicago: Children's Press.

Hammond, A. (1995). *Art works: Cartooning.* San Diego, CA: Thunder Bay Press.

Lightfoot, M. (1993). *Cartooning for kids.* Toronto: Greey de Pencier Books.

Scott, E. (1993). *Funny papers: Behind the scenes of the comics.* New York: William Morrow & Co. Library.

Smith, C. (1997). *How to draw cartoons.* Milwaukee, WI: Gareth Stevens.

Smith, F. (1997). *I can draw comics and cartoons.* New York: Little Simon.

Web sites

http://www.unitedmedia.com/ncs/ncs.html
Cartoonists Society, Natl.

http://www.cartooncorner.com
Cartoon Corner

Carving

Books

Butz, R. (1991). *How to carve wood: A book of projects and techniques.* Newtown, CT: Taunton Press.

Esterly, D. (1998). *Grinling Gibbons and the art of carving.* New York: Harry N. Abrams Inc.

Onians, D. (1997). *Essential woodcarving techniques.* New York: Sterling Publications.

Pye, C. (1995). *Woodcarving: Tools, materials and equipment.* New York: Sterling Publications.

Web site

http://www.tiac.net/users/rtrudel/newc.html
New England Wood Carvers

Collage

Books

Brown, M. D., & Metzger, P. (1998). *Realistic collage step by step.* Cincinnati, OH: North Light Books.

Carle, E. (1998). *You can make a collage: A very simple how-to book.* Palo Alto, CA: Klutz Press.

Carver, J. (1997). *Collage from seeds, leaves and flowers.* Newton Abbot, Devon, England: David & Charles.

Larbalestier, S. (1995). *The art and craft of collage.* San Francisco: Chronicle Books.

Pearce, A., Burton, S., Butler, S., & Copp, G. (1997). *The crafter's complete guide to collage.* New York: Watson-Guptill Publications.

Stocks, S., & Fairclough, C. (1994). *Collage.* Cincinnati, OH: Thomson Learning.

Web sites

www.eric-carle.com
Eric Carles' Official Web site

http://www.meininger.com/ArtEdResPages/PaperCollage.html
Paper Collage

http://post-dogmatist-arts.net/museum/collage/list.htm
The International Museum of Collage at the Ontological Museum Costume

Costume

Books

Anderson, B., & Anderson, C. (1998). *Costume design.* San Diego, CA: HBJ College & School Division.

Davies, S. (1997). *Costume language: A dictionary of dress terms.* New York: Drama Publishers.

Dearing, S. (1992). *Elegantly frugal costumes: The poor man's do-it-yourself costume maker's guide.* Colorado Spring, CO: Meriwether Publishing.

Govier, J., & Davies, G. (1996). *Create your own stage costumes.* Portsmouth, NJ: Heinemann.

Ingham, R. (1992). *The costume designer's handbook: A complete guide for amateur and professional costume designers.* Portsmouth, NJ: Heinemann.

Kidd, M. T. (1996). *Stage costume step-by-step: The complete guide to designing and making stage costumes for all major drama periods and genres from classical through time.* Cincinnati, OH: Betterway Publications.

Web sites

http://www.interlog.com/~gwhite/ttt/mtmainpg.html
The Museum for Textiles

http://members.aol.com/nebula5/costume.html
The Costume Page

http://ddi.digital.net/~milieux/costume.html
The Costume Site

http://www.milieux.com/costume/
Milieux: The Costume Site

http://www.museumofcostume.co.uk/
The Museum of Costume

Diorama

Books

Dodge, V. (1993). *Making miniatures: In ½ scale.* Newton Abbot, Devon, England: David & Charles.

Paine, S. (1994). *How to build dioramas.* Waukesha, WI: Kalmbach Publishing Company.

Schleicher, R. (1990). *Making dollhouses and dioramas: An easy approach using kits and ready-made parts.* Mineola, NY: Dover Publications.

Web site

http://westwood.fortunecity.com/macy/68/wenzel.htm
The Art of Making Dioramas

Graph

Books

Bryant-Mole, K. (1994). *Charts and graphs.* Tulsa, OK: EDC Publications.

Henry, G. T. (1995). *Graphing data: Techniques for display and analysis.* Mill Valley, CA: Sage Publications.

Software

Graph Action Plus CD-ROM
Tom Snyder Productions
80 Coolidge Hill Road
Watertown, MA 02472
Phone: (800) 342-0236

The Graph Club CD-ROM
Tom Snyder Productions
80 Coolidge Hill Road
Watertown, MA 02472
Phone: (800) 342-0236

Inspiration: Inspire Students to Develop Ideas and Organize Thinking
Tom Snyder Productions
80 Coolidge Hill Road
Watertown, MA 02472
Phone: (800) 342-0236

Web sites

http://scrtec.org/track/tracks/s00810.html
Graphing in the Information Age

http://chemed.chem.purdue.edu/~genchem/lab/datareports
Making a Graph on Graph Paper

Map

Books

Chapman, G. (1993). *Maps and Mazes: A first guide to mapmaking.* Brookfield, CT: Millbrook Press.

Ganeri, A. (1995). *Maps and mapmaking: Facts, things to make, activities.* Danbury, CT: Franklin Watts Inc.

Ganieri, A. (1998). *The story of maps and navigation.* New York: Oxford University Press Childrens Books.

Haslam, A., & Taylor, B. (1996). *Maps*. Chicago: World Book Inc.

Sobel, D. (1998). *Mapmaking with children: Sense of place education for the elementary years.* Portsmouth, NJ: Heinemann.

LaPierre, Y. (1996). *Mapping a changing world.* Palm Beach, FL: Lickle Publishing Incorporated.

Taylor, B. (1993). *Maps and mapping: Geography facts and experiments.* New York: Kingfisher Books.

Software

Mapmaker's Toolkit CD-ROM
Tom Snyder Productions
80 Coolidge Hill Road
Watertown, MA 02472
Phone: (800) 342-0236

Neighborhood MapMachine CD-ROM
Tom Snyder Productions
80 Coolidge Hill Road
Watertown, MA 02472
Phone: (800) 342-0236

Web sites

http://www.usgs.gov
United States Geological Survey

http://www.utenn.edu/uwa/vpps/ur/ut2kids/maps/map.html
Mapmaker, Mapmaker, Make Me a Map

http://www-nais.ccm.nrcan.gc.ca/schoolnet/teachkit/carto/htmle
Fundamentals of Cartography

Mobile

Books

Bawden, J. (1996). *Mobile magic: Innovative ideas for airborne accessories, over 80 creations and inspirations.* Dayton, OH: Lorenz Books.

Pinder, P. (1997). *How to make mobiles.* Grants Pass, OR: Search Press Ltd.

Sevaly, K. (1994). *Mobiles*. Riverside, CA: Teacher's Friend Publications, Inc.

Tibor (1997). *You can make mobiles*. Chicago: Allen & Unwin.

Williams, G. R. (1969). *Making mobiles*. White Plains, NY: Emerson Books, Inc.

Williams, M. (1994). *Magnificent Mobiles*. New York: Book Sales.

Web site

http://www.bconnex.net/~jarea/artists/calder.htm
KinderArt-Alexander Calder

Mural

Books

Capek, M. (1996). *Murals: Cave, cathedral, to street*. Minneapolis, MN: Lerner Publications Co.

Seligman, P. (1988). *Painting murals: Images, ideas, and techniques*. Cincinnati, OH: North Light Books.

Vasquez, S., (1998). *The school mural*. Milwaukee, WI: Raintree.

Software

Eureka! I Can Draw
Nu.Millenia Inc.
16868 Via Del Campo Court, Suite 200
San Diego, CA 92127
Phone: (800) 966-5437

Web site

http://www.muralart.com/
MuralArt.com

Photograph

Books

Gibbons, G. (1997). *Click: A book about cameras and taking pictures*. Boston, MA: Little Brown & Co.

King, D. (1994). *My first photography book.* London, England: Dorling Kindersley Publishers.

Oxolade, C. (1997). *Cameras.* Dayton, OH: Lorenz Books.

Price, S. (1997). *Click: Fun with photography.* Northampton, MA: Sterling Publications.

Software

Better Photography Learning to See Creatively
DiAmar Interactive Corp.
600 University St., Suite 1701
Seattle, WA 98101
Phone: (800) 234-2627
Internet: http://www.diamar.com

Web sites

http://www.primenet.com/~sos/photopage.html
Bob's Photo Page

http://www.library.arizona.edu/branches/ccp/ccphome.html
Center for Creative Photography

http://www.88.com/exposure/index.htm
Exposure—A Beginner's Guide To Photography

http://www.kodak.com:80/ciHome/photography/bPictures
Kodak Guide to Better Pictures

http://www.news:rec.photo.darkroom
rec.photo.darkroom

http://photo.net/photo
photo.net

Poster

Books

Friedl, F. (1998). *Typography: An encyclopedic survey of type design and techniques throughout history.* New York: Black Dog & Leventhal Publishing.

Timmers, M. (1998). *The power of the poster.* London, England: Victoria & Albert Museum.

Williams, R. (1994). *The non-designer's design book: Design and typographic principles for the visual novice.* Berkeley, CA: Peachpit Printing.

Williams, R. (1998). *The non-designer's type book: Insights and techniques for creating professional-level type.* Berkeley, CA: Peachpit Printing.

Web sites

http://aspp.org/education/poster.htm
How to Make a Great Poster

http://desktoppublishing.com/design.html
Graphic Design Links of Interest to Graphic Artists

Quilt

Books

Clark, M. C. (1995). *Story quilts and how to make them.* Northampton, MA: Sterling Publishing.

Florence, J. (1995). *Scrap quilts and how to make them.* Mineola, NY: Dover Publications.

Fons, M., & Porter, L. (1993). *Quilter's complete guide.* Birmingham, AL: Oxmoor House.

Heim, J., & Hansen, G. (1998). *Free stuff for quilters on the Internet.* Concord, CA: C & T Publishing.

Pahl, E. (Ed.) (1997). *The quilter's ultimate visual guide: From A to Z—hundreds of tips and techniques for successful quiltmaking.* Enmaus, PA: Rodale Printing.

Simms, A. (1996). *How not to make a prize-winning quilt.* Concord, CA: C & T Publishing.

Webster, M. D. (1992). *Quilts: Their story and how to make them.* Detroit, MI: Omnigraphics.

Web site

http://ttsw.com/MainQuiltingPage.html
World Wide Quilting Page

Sculpture

Books

Lanteri, E. (1985). *Modeling and sculpting animals.* Mineola, NY: Dover Publications.

Lanteri, E. (1985). *Modeling and sculpting the human figure.* Mineola, NY: Dover Publications.

Nigrosh, L. I. (1992). *Sculpting clay.* Tuscaloosa, AL: Davis Publications.

Rich, J. C. (1988). *The materials and methods of sculpture.* Mineola, NY: Dover Publications.

Web sites

http://www.sculptor.org/
Sculptor.Org

http://www.sculpturecenter.org/index.htm
The Sculpture Center

CHAPTER V

Oral Products

Products that rely solely on verbal, spoken, and unwritten means of communicating knowledge fall within this category. Oral products include but are not limited to:

Audio Tape	Oral Report
Commentary	Presentation
Debate	Readings
Description	Seminar
Discussion	Show and Tell
Interview	Speeches
Lecture	Storytelling

Contained within this chapter are in-depth profiles of six oral products. The definitions, titles of experts, types, words to know, helpful hints, exemplary producers, community resources, and quotes to inspire are provided for each of these products. Students should add to and expand these listings as they encounter new ideas and information in their research and product development process. Grids, which list the components, characteristics, and basic materials of each product, are also included along with examples of authentic products created by students. In addition, a bibliography containing books, web sites, and software specific to oral products is provided at the end of this chapter.

Product: Debate

Definition: Form of oral controversy consisting of the systematic presentation of opposing arguments on a selected topic.

Title of Expert: Debater

Types of Debate:

Academic	Lincoln-Douglas
Audience Decision	Mock Trial
Congressional	One on One
Cross-Questioning	Open Forum
Decision by Judges	Parliamentary
Decisionless	Presidential
Heckling	Single Critic Judge
Judicial	Town Hall

Words to Know:

Affirmative	Fallacy
Analogy	Flow Chart
Analysis	Forensics
Argument	Hierarchy
Assertion	Inductive Reasoning
Brief	Interview
Burden of Communication	Issue
Burden of Proof	Judge
Burden of Rebuttal	Leading Question
Case	Negative
Cause	Observation
Claim	Open Questions
Clash	Outline
Constructive Speed	Prima Facie Case
Contention	Probe Questions
Counter Proposal	Proof
Counter Warrant	Proposition
Critical Thinking	Quote
Cross Examine	Reasoning
Data	Rebuttal
Deductive Reasoning	Refutation
Deliberate	Research
Delivery	Resolution
Direct Question	Sign

Ethics	Time Limits
Evidence	Tournament

Helpful Hints:

- Sort important evidence.
- Listen to your opponent carefully.
- Enhance your skills in seeing logical connections.
- Learn to react to new ideas quickly.
- Develop a convincing manner of speech and employ principles of effective speaking.
- Research your topic thoroughly.
- Support your positions with proof.
- Consider all alternatives.
- Be conservative in your interpretations. Do not exaggerate.
- Examples and authorities cited must be familiar to the audience.
- Select propositions that deal with a controversial subject.

Exemplary Producers:

Henry Clay	Abraham Lincoln
Robert Dole	Peggy Noonan
Stephens Arnold Douglas	Ross Perot
Geraldine Ferraro	Robert Taft
Robert Hayne	Daniel Webster
Molly Ivans	

Community Resources: Debate Team, Forensics Teacher, Judges, Lawyers, Speech/Communication Teacher

Quotes to Inspire:

> "Freedom is hammered out on the anvil
> of discussion, dissent, and debate."
>
> —Hubert H. Humphrey

> "It is not he who gains the exact point in dispute
> who scores most in controversy—
> but he who has shown the better temper."
>
> —Samuel Butler

> "It is better to debate a question without settling it
> than to settle a question without debating it."
>
> —Jeseph Joubert

Product Criteria Grid

Product: Debate

Components	Characteristics	Basic Materials
Proposition	• Controversial, appropriate to audience and participants, interesting	Dictionary Experts Index Cards Internet Paper Pencil Resource Books Speaking Guides Stop Watch
Opening	• Clearly stated, well-planned, relevant to proposition, main points emphasized	
Argument	• Orderly, relevant to proposition, well-supported, significant	
Rebuttal	• Organized, clearly stated, thought-provoking, significant to case	
Closing Remarks	• Comprehensive, summary of key points, well-planned, thorough	

Product: Discussion

Definition: Conversation that results when two or more individuals gather together to share information and opinions on a topic or to think through a problem.

Title of Expert: Discusser/Discussant

Types of Discussion:

Bull Session	Open
Colloquium	Oratory
Committee	Panel
Conference	Parley
Consultation	Parliamentary
Debate	Policy-Determining
Dialogue	Pourparler
Extemporaneous	Private
Focus Group	Public
Formal	Radio
Forum	Roundtable
Group	Study Group
Hearing	Symposium
Impromptu	Teach-In
Informal	Televised
Intercollegiate	Trialogue

Words to Know:

Advocate	Language
Agenda	Leadership
Analogy	Listen
Analysis	Moderator
Argue	Opinion
Chairman	Oral
Cite	Parliamentary
Clarifier	Participation
Closure	Persuasion
Compromise	Point
Conversation	Point of View
Criteria	Problem
Criticism	Procedure
Delivery	Quotation
Details	Reasoning
Dialogue	Rebuttal

Discourse	Reflection
Exchange	Socratic Method
Explanation	Solution
Facilitator	Sources
Forum	Stenographer
Gag Rule	Topic
Investigation	Transcript
Issue	Values
Justification	Visual Aid

Helpful Hints:

- Your language must be clear.
- Organize your ideas before speaking.
- Make sure you have enough facts to justify your belief.
- The subject selected to discuss must raise a recognizable problem … it should be worthy of discussing.
- The problem should be suited to the group's interest, knowledge, and size as well as the allotted time.
- Converse with others about the subject prior to formal discussion.
- Prepare an outline.
- Select a seating arrangement that best suits the discussion type.
- Impose rules and procedures for discussion.
- Make sure all parties in the discussion equally participate.
- Keep the discussion relevant.
- Develop good listening habits. Listen to learn and understand.
- Enter into the discussion when you have something relevant and useful to offer.
- Think before you speak.
- Speak intelligibly.

Exemplary Producers:

Barbara Boxer	Newt Gingrich
Winston Churchill	Larry King
Bill Clinton	Jay Leno
Robert Dole	Bill Maher
W. E. B. Dubois	Oprah Winfrey

Community Resources: Forensics Teacher, Policy Makers, Professor of Political Science, Professor of Speech/Communication

"It's an indulgence to sit in a room and discuss your beliefs
as if they were a juicy piece of gossip."

—Lillian Hellman

"A philosopher who is not taking part in discussions
is like a boxer who never goes into the ring."

—Ludwig Wittgenstein

"Opinions are formed in a process of open discussion and public debate,
and where no opportunity for the forming of opinions exists,
there may be moods—moods of the masses and moods of individuals,
the latter no less fickle and unreliable than the former—but no opinion."

—Hannah Arendt

"Discussion is an exchange of knowledge;
argument an exchange of ignorance."

—Robert Quillen

"Good communication is as stimulating as black coffee,
and just as hard to sleep after."

—Anne Morrow Lindbergh

Product Criteria Grid

Product: Discussion

Components	Characteristics	Basic Materials
Topic	• Relevant, of immediate importance	Chairs Chalkboard Chart Microphone Name Tags Overhead Paper Pencil Resources Table Water
Problem (optional)	• Has a feasible solution, thoroughly analyzed	
Discussants	• Knowledgeable of topic, logical, well-informed, participating, objective	
Recorder	• Accurate, precise, prompt, unbiased	
Room Arrangement	• Conducive to discussion type and number of participants, well-lit, comfortable, free from distractions	
Resolution/ Recommendation	• Based on evidence, reached by majority consensus, timely, feasible	
Visual Aids (optional)	• Neat, visible, enhances key points	

Product: Interview

Definition: An interaction in which one person requests information and the other supplies it. Usually initiated for a specific purpose and focused on some particular content with elimination of extraneous material.

Title of the Expert: Interviewer

Types of Interviews:

Broadcast	Panel
Clinical	Telephone
E-mail	Via Satellite
Face-to-Face	Written
Legal	

Words to Know:

Attitude	Motive
Bias	Off-the-Record
Body Language	On-the-Record
Expression	Open-Ended Question
Facial	Opinions
Fact	Point of View
Fiction	Postures
Gestures	Probe
Goal	Question
Lavalieres	Reporter
Leading	Source
Leading Question	Tape Recorder
Loaded Question	Video Tape
Microphone	

Helpful Hints:

- Choose an environment where sounds/scenes enhance the interview.
- Anticipate unexpected noises and other distractions.
- Control your pace.
- Do your homework and prepare questions in advance.
- Be straightforward.
- When necessary, interrupt the interviewee tactfully.
- In case you may need more information, ask where you can reach the interviewee later.
- Avoid questions that can be answered simply "yes" or "no."
- Ask permission to audio- or videotape, if that is your intention.

- Consider the order in which you will ask selected questions. Save the best questions for last.

Exemplary Producers:

Carl Bernstein	Bill Moyers
David Brinkley	Edward R. Murrow
Ralph Ellison	Diane Sawyer
Oriana Fallaci	Maria Shriver
David Frost	Susan Stamberg
Alex Haley	Mike Wallace
Larry King	Barbara Walters
Jim Lehrer	Oprah Winfrey
Robert MacNeil	Bob Woodward

Community Resources: Communication/Speech Teacher; Local Media/Newspaper, Radio, TV; Professor of Broadcast Journalism; Public Relations Director

Quotes to Inspire:

"The best interviews—like the best biographies—
should sing the strangeness and variety of the human race."

—Lynn Barber

"Questions are never indiscreet. Answers sometimes are."

—Oscar Wilde

Product Criteria Grid

Product: Interview

Components	Characteristics	Basic Materials
Planning	• Well-organized, specific purpose defined, arrangements made in advance	Camcorder Computer Microphone Note Cards
Questions	• Interesting, related to purpose, varied, planned in advance, carefully selected/considered, appropriate order	Paper Pencil Tape Recorder Tripod
Location	• Quiet, free from distractions, comfortable, convenient	Video Tape

Product: Presentation

Definition: The act of conveying information in an appropriate manner to an intended audience.

Title of Expert: Presenter, Speaker, Lecturer

Types of Presentations:

Business	Informative
Conference	Multimedia
How-To	Oral

Words to Know:

Agenda	Impromptu
Anecdotes	Interactive
Arrangement	Microphone
Audible	Models
Audience	Overhead
Audio-Visual Equipment	Pace
Body Language	Pause
Chalkboard	Podium
Distraction	Posture
Environment	Props
Expressiveness	Slides
Facial Expression	Stage
Flip Chart	Style
Format	Tempo
Forum	Visual Aids
Gestures	Volume
Ideas	

Helpful Hints:

- Construct an outline of what the presentation will cover.
- Be energetic, for this will capture your audience's attention.
- Avoid jargon or slang.
- Remember that too many ideas presented too quickly can be confusing.
- Stick to the important points.
- Talk to the audience.
- Various types of visual aids can be used to emphasize major points.
- If possible, get to the room ahead of the audience to examine the room arrangement and check equipment.
- Keep in mind that audiences can be diverse … pitch to a general level.

- Be sure to define terms and explain difficult concepts.
- Consider having a question-and-answer period at the conclusion of the presentation.
- Thank the audience.

Exemplary Producers:

Madeline Albright	Ralph Nader
Hillary Rodham Clinton	Ross Perot
Elizabeth Dole	Colin Powell
Malcolm Forbes	Louis Rukizer
Bill Gates	Norman Schwartzkoff
Lee Iacoca	Roger Wagner
Mary Kay	William C. Westmoreland

Community Resources: Forensics Teacher/Speech Teacher, Toastmasters, Media Specialist, Business Persons, Presidents of Local Businesses/Associations

Quotes to Inspire:

"Proper words in proper places make the definition of style."

—Jonathon Swift

"To sum up, an oral presentation deserves
a somewhat different treatment from a written paper,
because even the most mature technical talk
is usually a grown-up version of 'show and tell.'"

—Herbert B. Michaelson

The Scribe's Son

by Marni Scotten

 *Marni Scotten is a 15-year-old ninth grader attending Cate High School in Carpinteria, CA. She has two older brothers named Brent and Chris. Her hobbies include swimming, reading, and writing. In addition, she also plays volleyball and is the starting pitcher on her school's varsity softball team. She created this independent study program when she was a seventh grader at Ojai Valley School in Ojai, CA.*

Upon learning that an independent study program was to be initiated at my school, I was excited and curious. It was the first time our school had offered such a program, and I was pleased to be one of the four students selected to participate. In our first few meetings, the requirements for the project were discussed. To assist us in this process, our teacher asked us to write five things that were of interest to us.

My selection was Ancient Egypt because their culture had always intrigued me. Archaeology immediately came to mind, but my focus of study turned to hieroglyphs instead. The next step was to select a way to present the project. It was determined that we should make the presentation as fun and creative as possible. Since my talent lies in writing, an historical fiction story appealed to me along with a short presentation on hieroglyphs.

It was necessary to collect all the information on hieroglyphs and Ancient Egypt's culture by using the Internet and many books. Once enough information was gathered, the writing process began. It took several drafts until the story was completed. My teacher, the students in my group, and my parents helped me to revise it and offered constructive criticism.

After completing the story, the next step was to shape a presentation for the hieroglyphs and create an activity for the sixth-grade class. Clay pots were created like the ones used to carry food and water when a person was buried in a mastaba, or tomb. The sixth-grade class was given a paper that had a translation of the English alphabet into the Egyptian one. They wrote on the clay pots in hieroglyphs using toothpicks.

The project turned out well and brought much enjoyment. The advice I would give to another student would be to monitor your work schedule. Much to my surprise, the project was due in two months, which seemed like a lot of time. I soon discovered that even by meeting three days a week, there were many small details that still needed to be accomplished during the last week. Consequently, I was left scrambling to get things done at the last minute. I really learned a lot from this project. After reading and writing about Ancient Egypt for two months, more information was gained than expected. In addition, I learned how to put a big project together, and, although it was hard work, I would do it again. In closing, my advice is "Do or do not; there is no try." —Yoda, from *The Empire Strikes Back*.

Product Criteria Grid

Product: Presentation

Components	Characteristics	Basic Materials
Title	• Relevant to content/topic, intriguing	Books/Internet
Content	• Appropriate to audience, significant accurate	Computer Index Cards Microphone Overhead Projector
Voice	• Audible, natural, appropriate inflection and tone	Paper Pencil Podium
Body Language	• Professional, use of movement (i.e., hand gestures, expression) for emphasis, eye contact with audience	Presentation Software Transparency
Visual Aids (optional)	• Clear, neat, concise, visible, appropriate size, accurate, enhancing	

Product: Speech

Definition: A talk or public address on a specific topic to inform or influence an audience.

Title of the Expert: Orator, Speaker

Types of Speeches:

Ceremonial	Informative
Congratulatory	Introductory
Deliberative	Jeremiad
Demonstrative	Nominating
Epideictic	Oration
Eulogy	Persuasive
Extemporaneous	Point of View
Forensic	Political
Humorous	Rebuttal
Illustrative	Recognition
Impromptu	Sermon

Words to Know:

Alliteration	Message
Analogy	Metaphor
Anecdote	Oratory
Antithesis	Parallelism
Articulation	Peroration
Audience	Persona
Auditor	Pitch
Chiasmus	Rate
Delivery	Refutation
Discourse	Rhetoric
Dissonance	Satire
Enthymene	Style
Exordium	Syllogism
Genre	Theme
Gester	Visual Aid
Imagery	Voice
Irony	Volume
Memorize	

Helpful Hints:

- Your message must be relevant to the audience.

- Rehearse out loud.
- Videotape or tape record yourself.
- Choose your words carefully. Avoid slang.
- Look at every person in the group or each section of the room at some time during your speech.
- Use appropriate body language.
- The tempo should be geared to topic and audience.
- If appropriate, use visual aids to enhance the content of your speech.

Exemplary Producers:

Aeschines
Spiro Agnew
Maya Angelou
Susan B. Anthony
John Bright
William Jennings Bryan
Edmund Burke
John Calvin
Fidel Castro
Cato the Elder
Shirley Chisholm
Winston Churchill
Cicero
Henry Clay
Bill Clinton
Corax of Syracuse
Crassus
Mario Cuomo
George Jacques Danton
Demosthenes
Elizabeth Dole
Frederick Douglass
Angelina Emily
Edward Everett
Charles James Fox

Patrick Henry
Isocrates
Jesse Jackson
Barbara Jordan
Martin Luther King
Louis Kossuth
Charles Kuralt
Abraham Lincoln
Rosa Luxemburg
Nelson Mandela
Daniel O'Connell
Tip O'Neill
Peggy Noonan
Wendell Phillips
Eleanor Roosevelt
Franklin D. Roosevelt
Seneca
Anna Howard Shaw
Philip Dormer Stanhope
Elizabeth Cady Stanton
Tisias
Booker T. Washington
Daniel Webster
Woodrow Wilson

Community Resources: Forensics Teacher, Newscasters, Politicians, Political Science Teacher, Professor of Speech/Communication, Toastmasters Club

Quotes to Inspire:

"The right word may be effective,
but no word was ever as effective
as a rightly timed pause."

—Mark Twain

"The best impromptu speeches
are the ones written well in advance."

—Ruth Gordon

O the orator's joys!
To inflate the chest to roll the thunder of the voice out from the ribs and throat,
To make the people rage, weep, hate, desire, with
Yourself,
To lead America—to quell America with a great
Tongue

—Walt Whitman

Product Criteria Grid

Product: Speech

Components	Characteristics	Basic Materials
Title	• Relevant to topic, original, captures audience interest	Camcorder Computer Microphone Overhead Paper Pencil Podium Screen Speech Guide Books Tape Recorder Video Tape
Topic	• Appropriate to audience, original, significant	
Opening	• Captures attention, provides an overview	
Voice	• Pleasant, audible, clear, natural	
Body Language	• Appropriate, professional, relaxed	
Closing	• Summarizes main points, leaves listener satisfied	
Visual Aids (optional)	• Enhance speech, clearly visible to all audience members, neat, consideration of design principles and elements (i.e., balance, emphasis, variety, contrast, etc.)	

Product: Storytelling

Definition: The oral interpretation of something heard, read, witnessed, dreamt, or experienced.

Title of Expert: Storyteller; Griot

Types of Storytelling:

Adventure	Nature
Flannel Board	Pantomime
Folk Tales	Patriotic
Historical	Puppet
Humorous	Real-Life
Legends	Round Robin
Mysteries	Song
Myths	

Words to Know:

Atmosphere	Middle
Beginning	Myth
Breathing	Parable
Elements	Pause
Ending	Posture
Enunciation	Props
Expression	Timing
Eye Contact	Tone
Fable	Voice
Folk tale	Volume
Legend	

Helpful Hints:

- Select a story appropriate to the occasion, interests, and ages of the audience.
- Commit the story to memory.
- Use appropriate body language and facial expressions.
- Use words and phrases applicable to the information conveyed.
- Employ intonation, pitch, stress, and juncture, and articulate clearly.
- Sit or stand close to your audience.
- Start with shorter, familiar stories and build to longer, more complex ones.
- Tape your story and listen to it critically.
- Utilize pauses wisely and don't be afraid of them.
- Use costumes and props to enhance the story.

Exemplary Producers:

Hans Christian Andersen	Papa Alonzo Leatherby
Maya Angelou	George MacDonald
Marc Batten	Richard Martin
Giovanni Boccaccio	Lee-Ellen Marvin
Geoffrey Chaucer	William Somerset Maughem
Roald Dahl	Nancy Schimmel
Isak Dinesen	Sir Walter Scott
Joe Hayes	Bob Shimer
Gail Herman	Isaac Bashevis Singer
Zora Neale Hurston	Mary Carter Smith
Eamon Kelly	Jan Steen
Hanif Kureishi	Eudora Welty
Charles Kuralt	Richard and Judy Young

Community Resources: English Teachers, Librarians, Local Storytellers, Storytelling Festivals

Quotes to Inspire:

"You are prepared to tell your story, then forget yourself.
You are the instrument; the story is the thing."
—Gudrum Thorne-Thomson

"In the end it is important that you should tell your story
in your own words with sincerity and enthusiasm."
—Barry McWilliams

"The first law of story-telling …
Every man is bound to leave a story better than he found it."
—Mrs. Humphrey Ward

Product Criteria Grid

Product: Storytelling

Components	*Characteristics*	*Basic Materials*
Title	• Relevant to theme/topic, concise, captures attention	Book Camcorder Computer Paper Pencil Props/Costumes (optional) Story Tape Recorder
Opening	• Captivating, attention-getting, introduces main characters, setting, subject matter	
Voice	• Appropriate to mood and characters of story, audible	
Gestures	• Within character, enhances story	
Facial Expressions	• Reflects mood and character, conveys appropriate feelings and emotions	
Props/Costumes (optional)	• Enhances story, not distracting	
Ending	• Satisfying, appropriate closers, thought-provoking, purpose of story evident	

Oral Resources
Debate

Books

Dunbar, R. E. (1994). *How to debate (Speak out, write on!)*. Danbury, CT: Franklin Watts Inc.

Erison, J., Murphy, J., & Zeuschner, R. (1987). *The debater's guide.* Carbondale, IL: Southern Illinois University Printing.

Oberg, B. C. (1995). *Forensics: The winner's guide to speech contests.* Colorado Springs, CO: Meriwether Publishing.

Phillips, L., Hicks, W., & Springer, D. (1996). *Basic debate.* Lincolnwood, IL: National Textbook Co.

Web sites

http://www.mindspring.com/~dbn/links-gen.html
Leslie's General Debate Links Page

http://www.puyallup.k12.wa.us/junior/ballou/sp_index.html
Mr. Peterson's Speech and Debate Classes

Discussion

Books

Gaunt-Leshinsky, J. (1995). *Authentic listening and discussion for advanced students.* Englewood Cliffs, NJ: Prentice-Hall.

Rabow, J. (1994). *William Fawcett Hill's learning through discussion.* Newbury Park, CA: Sage Publications.

Web site

http://ag.arizona.edu/aed/aed695a/using.htm
Using Discussion

Interview

Books

Barone, J. T. (1994). *Interviewing art and skill.* Needham Heights, MA: Allyn & Bacon.

McLaughlin, P. (1990). *How to interview: The art of asking questions.* Bellingham, WA: Self Counsel Press.

Yeschke, C. L. (1997). *The art of investigative interviewing: A human approach to testimonial evidence.* Woburn, MA: Butterworth-Heinemann.

Zimmerman, W. (1999). *How to tape instant oral biographies: Recording your family's life story in sound and sight.* White Hall, VA: Betterway Publications.

Web sites

http://espsun.space.swri.edu/interviews/howto.htm
How to Conduct a Good Interview

http://projects.edtech.sandi.net/memorial/exploring/3Interview
Interviewing

Presentation

Books

Heyden, N. (1997). *Stand and deliver: Giving business presentations.* White Plains, NY: Addison-Wesley.

Stevens, M. (1996). *How to be better at ... giving presentations.* Dover, NH: Kogan Page Limited.

Web sites

http://www.students.dsu.edu/goughe/academics/presentation.htm
Presentation Tips

http://www.minnwest.com/education/tips.html
Presentation Tips and Techniques

http://www.asp.org/asp1999/presguidelines.htm
Guidelines for the Preparation of Effective Presentations

Speech

Books

Otfinoski, S. (1997). *Speaking up, speaking out: A kid's guide to making speeches, oral reports, and conversation.* Brookfield, CT: Millbrook Press.

Ryan, M. (1996). *How to give a speech (Speak out, write on!).* New York: Franklin Watts.

Web sites

http://www.toastmasters.org/
Toastmasters International

http://speeches.com/index.shtml
"Unaccustomed as I Am ..." the Web Pages of David Slack Speech Writing

Storytelling

Books

Casady, M., & Zapel, T. O. (1994). *The art of storytelling: Creative ideas for preparation and performance.* Colorado Springs, CO: Meriwether Publishing.

Davis, D. (1993). *Telling your own stories: For family and classroom storytelling, public speaking, and personal journaling.* Little Rock, AR: August House Publishing.

Hamilton, M., & Weiss, M. (1990). *Children tell stories: A teaching guide.* Katonah, NY: Richard C. Owen Publishing.

Hamilton, M. (1997). *Stories in my pocket: Tales kids can tell.* Golden, CO: Fulcrum Publishing.

Hayes, J. (1996). *Here comes the storyteller.* El Paso, TX: Cinco Puntos Printing.

MacDonald, M. R. (1993). *The storyteller's start-up book: Finding, learning, performing, and using folktales including twelve tellable tales.* Little Rock, AR: August House Publishing.

Mellon, N. (1998). *The art of storytelling.* Rockport, MA: Element.

Mooney, W. (1996). *The storyteller's guide: Storytellers share advice for the classroom, boardroom, showroom, podium, pulpit and center stage.* Little Rock, AR: August House Publishing.

Sierra, J. (1997). *The flannel board storytelling book.* New York: H. W. Wilson.

Web sites

http://www.state.lib.ut.us/story.htm
Storytime Resources

http://members.aol.com/storypage/index.htm
The Storytelling Home Page

CHAPTER VI

Performance Products

Performance products are those that communicate through action, movement, and execution, emphasizing kinesthetic integration. These products include but are not limited to:

Demonstration	Play
Skit	Dance
Dramatization	Musical Performance
Simulation	Puppet Show
Comedy Sketch	Monologue
Experiment	

This chapter includes detailed descriptions of seven selected performance products. Information relating to definitions, title of experts, types, words to know, helpful hints, exemplary producers, community resources, and quotes to inspire are provided. These listings provide a foundation upon which to begin your research. Feel free to add to these listings as you discover new information relating to the particular product. Grids that detail the components, characteristics, and basic materials necessary for each product are also displayed. Furthermore, authentic performance products created by students are highlighted. For additional information, a bibliography of books, web sites, and suggested software is included at the end of this chapter.

Product: Dance

Definition: Rhythmic movement of the body and feet, usually to music.

Title of the Expert: Dancer, Choreographer

Types of Dances:

Ballet	Jazz
Ballroom	Jitterbug
Belly	Lambada
Bolero	Line
Break Dance	Macharana
Cakewalk	Mazurka
Cancan	Minuet
Ceremonial	Modern
Cha-Cha	Pointe
Charleston	Polka
Classical	Pony
Clog	Reel
Communal	Ritual
Conga	Round
Cotillion	Shadow
Country-Western	Social
Disco	Square
Egyptian	Tango
Fandango	Tap
Flamenco	Twist
Folk	Two-Step
Fox-Trot	Waltz
Hop	Water

Words to Know:

Alignment	Improvision
Arrangement	Labanotation
Acrobat	Leap
Agility	Leotard
Audition	Movement
Balance	Premier
Ball Change	Premiere
Body Mechanics	Rhythm
Choreograph	Shuffle
Compose	Space

Coordination	Steps
Danseur	Stretch
Danseuse	Technique
Do-si-do	Transition
Entrechat	Turn
Grand Jete	

Helpful Hints:

- Make sure you know all the steps before performing.
- Select the dance type and music to the occasion.
- Stretch and warm-up before performing.
- Experiment with different combinations of steps.
- Be sure to have the appropriate foot apparel for the dance type.
- Select clothing that allows movement and is appropriate for the type of dance.
- Enroll in classes to perfect technique and performance skills.
- If you make a mistake, keep going with the next steps.
- Videotape yourself to analyze your strengths and weaknesses.
- Eat well and exercise regularly to maintain your strength and endurance.
- Learn to use imagery.
- Explore new ways of moving.

Exemplary Producers:

Alvin Ailey	José Arcadio Limon
Debbie Allen	Murray Louis
Jacque d'Amboise	Natalia Makarova
Fred Astaire	Peter Martins
Josephine Baker	Leonide Massine
George Balanchine	Donald McKayle
Mikhail Baryshnikov	Mark Morris
Ray Bolger	Vaslav Nijinsky
Erik Bruhn	Alwin Nikolais
Fernando Bujones	John George Noverre
Irene Castle	Rudolf Nureyev
Vernon Blythe Castle	Moses Pendleton
Gower Champion	Jules Perrot
Merce Cunningham	Marius Petipa
Serge Diaghilev	Pearl Primus
Isadora Duncan	Jerome Robbins
Katherine Dunham	Ginger Rogers
Andre' Eglevsky	Ted Shawn
Michel Fokine	Ruth St. Denis
Margot Fonteyn	Helen Tamiris

Bob Fosse
Martha Graham
Robert Helpmann
Gregory Hines
Doris Humphrey
Judith Jamison
Robert Joffrey
Kurt Jooss
Gene Kelly
Serge Lifar

Paul Taylor
Peter Ilich Tchaikovsky
Glen Tetley
Twyla Tharp
Anthony Tudor
Gaetan Vestris
Edward Villella
Galina Vlanova
Charles Weidman

Community Resources: Choreographers, Dance Studios, Dance Education Specialists, Professors of Dance, College and University Dance Programs

Quotes to Inspire:

"Nothing is more revealing than movement."

—Martha Graham

"We look at dance to impart sensation of living in an affirmation of life,
to energize the spectator into keener awareness of the vigor,
the mystery, the humor, the variety, and the wonder of life.
This is the function of the American dance."

—Martha Graham

"I do not know what the spirit of a philosopher could more wish to be than a good dancer.
For the dance is his ideal, also his fine art,
also the only kind of piety he knows, his 'divine service.'"

—Friedrich Nietzsche

Product Criteria Grid

Product: Speech

Components	Characteristics	Basic Materials
Type	• Corresponds to theme or topic	Appropriate Shoes Mat Mirror (optional) Music Tape Recorder
Movement	• Coordinated with music (if present), smooth transitions, accurate	
Music (optional)	• Appropriate to movements, enhances dance, appropriate for theme/mood	
Costume/Prop (optional)	• Enhances dance, nonconstricting, representative of theme	
Lighting (optional)	• Enhances dance, properly positioned	

Product: Experiment

Definition: A test under controlled conditions that is conducted to demonstrate a known truth, examine the validity of a hypothesis, or determine the efficacy of something previously untried.

Title of the Expert: Scientist/Researcher

Types of Experiments:

Behavioral Science	Electronic
Biological Science	Exploratory
Consumer/Social Science	Physical Science
Controlled	Practical
Demonstration	Scientific

Words to Know:

Analyze	Null
Conclusion	One-Way Analysis
Constants	Phenomena
Control Group	Placebo
Correlation	Prediction
Data	Procedures
Dependent Variable	Qualitative
Descriptive	Quantitative
Design	Record
Empirical	Repeated Trials
Experimental Group	Research
Graph	Results
Hypothesis	Sample
Independent Variable	Scientific Method
Instrument	Significance
Interaction	Statistics
Interval	Stimulus
Investigation	Subjects
Laboratory	T-Test
Main Effects	Treatment
Methodology	Validity
Nominal Variation	

Helpful Hints:

• For the beginner, experiments with one independent variable are suggested.

- Put results of your experiment in a diagram, chart, or table.
- Design an experiment in an area that interests you.
- Refine your procedures prior to conducting the experiment.
- Expect the unexpected.
- Make certain you have considered all steps of the Scientific Method.
- Make notes of ways to improve your experiment.
- Maintain ethical standards.
- Use appropriate safety procedures.

Exemplary Producers:

Sir Frances Bacon	Edward Jenner
William Beaumont	Otto Lilienthal
Alexander Graham Bell	James Lind
George Washington Carver	Andre Lwoff
Genry Cavendish	Gregor Johann Mendel
Sir George Cayley	Albert Abraham Michelson
Marie Curie	Samuel Finley Breese Morse
Thomas Edison	Ralph Nader
Albert Einstein	Sir Isaac Newton
Gertrude Elion	Blaise Pascal
Enrico Fermi	Louis Pasteur
Benjamin Franklin	Ivan Petrovich Pavlov
Sigmund Freud	August Piccard
Luigi Galvani	Ernest Rutherford
Alexander Freiherr	Burrhus Frederick Skinner
von Humboldt	Warner VanBraun

Community Resources: Science Teacher, Physicians, University Professors, Laboratory Technicians, Water Purification Managers

Quotes to Inspire:

"No amount of experimentation can ever prove me right;
a single experiment can prove me wrong."

—Albert Einstein

"The great tragedy of science—the slaying of a beautiful hypothesis by an ugly fact."

—Aldous Huxley

"There is one thing even more vital to science than intelligent methods;
and that is, the sincere desire to find out the truth, whatever it may be."

—Charles Sanders Pierce

Lung Capacity Experiment
by Krystal Kennedy

 *Krystal Kennedy is in the sixth grade at Presbyterian Christian School in Hattiesburg, MS. She is a competitive gymnast and also enjoys reading poetry and playing basketball. Her favorite school subject is science.*

After reading a book about science fair projects and talking with my mom and step-dad, who are both in the medical field, I became interested in seeing if age and size matters in lung capacity. Instead of reading a book on lung capacity, I decided to conduct an experiment. I also felt that an experiment would be the best way to answer questions about factors that affect a person's lung capacity. It was also determined that charts and graphs would be an effective way to show how age and size affects capacity.

In order to conduct the experiment, a spirometer that measures lung capacity was needed. My mother, who is a nurse, was able to bring one home from the hospital. A booklet that came with the spirometer provided a lot of useful information for my research. This booklet explained how to use the spirometer, and it also gave averages of females' and males' lung capacity. From this information, I developed a hypothesis that stated that a person's lung capacity increases with age and size. Different age and size people were selected for the study sample, and their lung capacity was measured using the spirometer. All data were then recorded on a chart. Results revealed that lung capacity does increase with a person's size and that it peaks around age 20 and slowly decreases from there.

In the process of researching lung capacity and conducting this experiment, I learned a lot about health. This experiment and its results were shared at the school science fair and with my family. A display using charts and graphs was also created to visually show the results of this experiment. At the elementary school science fair, this project obtained second place, which qualified me to show my project at the high school science fair.

A lot was learned from conducting this experiment. For example, age and size really does matter in a person's lung capacity. All students should try to explore things they don't know and want to learn more about. I encourage others to try conducting experiments and see what all the fun is about.

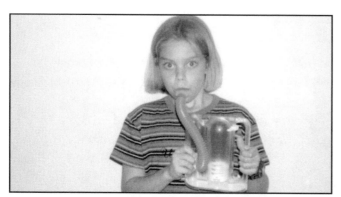

Krystal demonstrates how to use the spirometer.

Product Criteria Grid

Product: Experiment

Components	Characteristics	Basic Materials
Statement of Problem	• Clearly stated, significant	Calculator Computer Lab Coat Paper Pencil Safety Goggles Testing Instrument Test Tubes
Hypothesis	• Relevant to problem, direction stated as to predicted outcome	
Data Collection	• Clear explanation of methods to be used, thorough, description of subjects, selection of appropriate instrument(s), comprehensive review of literature and/or related research	
Test of Hypotheses	• Detailed description of procedures, appropriate statistical methods (if applicable)	
Results	• Restatement of hypothesis, acknowledgment of the acceptance or rejection of the hypothesis, data adequately analyzed and discussed, statement of recommendations	

Product: Monologue

Definition: A prolonged talk by a single speaker, usually on a specific topic.

Title of Expert: Actor, Monologist

Types of Monologues:

Dramatic	Humor
Historical	Political

Words to Know:

Actions	Pitch
Character	Plot
Climax	Pointing
Concentration	Progressions
Costume	Relaxation
Dialect	Rhythm
Diction	Role
Entrance	Script
Facial Expression	Space
Gesture	Stage Direction
Improvisation	Tempo
Mood	Timbre
Movement	Timing
Narrative	Vocal Techniques
Pace	Volume
Pause	

Helpful Hints:

- Find material that you really want to perform.
- Develop the personality for the character.
- Employ the appropriate physical actions and facial expressions.
- Determine the voice qualities of pitch, tone, volume, rate, and clarity of diction.
- Anything written in the first person singular is worth considering for material.
- You may have to make material by cutting, editing, and piecing it together.
- Create monologues through improvisation and record them on tape.
- Remember, the space in which you perform can be both an opportunity and a limitation.
- Costumes and props can be used to enhance performance.

Exemplary Producers:

Robert Charles Benchly   Cornelia Otis Skinner
Robert Browning   Lily Tomlin
Henry Fonda   James Whitmore
Spalding Gray   Emlyn Williams
Julie Harris   Lanford Wilson
Hal Holbrook   Edward Young
Edgar Lee Masters

Community Resources: Actor/Actress, Speech Teacher, Professors of Drama

Quotes to Inspire:

"There is no such thing as conversation. It is an illusion.
There are only intersecting monologues, that is all."

—Rebecca West

"Show me a character whose life arouses my curiosity,
and my flesh begins crawling with suspense."

—Fawn M. Brodie

Product Criteria Grid

Product: Monologue

Components	Characteristics	Basic Materials
Title	• Concise, appealing to audience	Costume Lighting (optional) Microphone Paper Pencil Props Resources Script
Content	• Appropriate for intended audience, engaging, descriptive vocabulary	
Beginning	• Introduces character and setting, captivates audience	
Voice	• Audible, appropriate to character, clear, suitable pace, accurate dialect for person, place, and time	
Body Language/Facial Expressions	• Corresponds with character and dialogue, used to emphasize selected points, not distracting	
Appearance/Costume	• Historically accurate, enhances character	
Props (optional)	• Suitable for character, enhances performance, realistic	
Ending	• Satisfying, summarizes main points, sense of closure, thought-provoking	

Product: Musical Performance

Definition: The art of producing aesthetically organized sound and silence within time and space.

Title of Expert: Musician

Types of Musical Performance:

Band	Orchestra
Choir	Parades
Choral	Quartet
Concert	Quintet
Duet	Recital
Ensemble	Serenade
Instrumental	Sextet
Jazz	Solo
Marching Band	Stage
Musical	Trio
Music Video	Vocal

Words to Know:

Accompaniment	Kinesthesis
Acoustic	Notation
Adagio	Percussion
Auditorium	Pitch
Brasses	Posture
Bravura	Practice
Breathing	Prelude
Competition	Presto
Concentration	Production Range
Conductor	Reed
Cue	Rehearsal
Finale	Rendition
Gig	Strings
Harmony	Tempo
Interlude	Transpose
Intermission	Tutti
Key	Warm-Up

Helpful Hints:

- Performances should present music of the best quality appropriate for the occasion.
- Practice is required for mastery.

- Limit the length of the performance to suit your audience.
- Scenery, if used, should complement the performance.
- Arrange the musical numbers in a meaningful sequence.

Exemplary Producers:

Louis Armstrong	Jimi Hendrix
William Basie	Sam Hopkins
The Beatles	Lena Horne
Chuck Berry	Whitney Houston
Sarah Caldwell	Jerry Lee Lewis
Ray Charles	Liberace
Eric Clapton	Little Richard
Van Cliburn	Henry Mancini
Nat King Cole	Barbara Mandrell
John Coltrane	Elvis Presley
Miles Davis	Jean-Pierre Rampal
Celine Dion	John Philip Sousa
Fats Domino	Ringo Starr
Tommy Dorsey	Isaac Stern
Duke Ellington	Barbra Streisand
Dizzy Gillespie	James Taylor
Woody Guthrie	George Thoroughgood
Coleman Hawkins	

Community Resources: Band/Orchestra Director, Conservatory, Musician, Music Teacher

Quotes to Inspire:

"Music, in performance, is a type of sculpture.
The air in the performance is sculpted into something."

—Frank Zappa

"Music is your own experience, your own thoughts, your wisdom.
If you don't live it, it won't come out of your horn.
They teach you there's a boundary line to music.
But, man, there's no boundary line to art."

—Charlie Parker

"Without music, life is a journey through a desert."

—Pat Conroy

"If you can walk, you can dance. If you can talk, you can sing."

—Zimbabwe Proverb

"True music must repeat the thought and aspirations of the people and the time. My people are Americans and my time is today."

—George Gershwin

"The history of a people is found in its songs."

—George Jellinek

"To compose music, all you have to do is remember a tune that nobody else has thought of."

—Robert Schumann

Product Criteria Grid

Product: Musical Performance

Components	Characteristics	Basic Materials
Title/Theme	• Relevant to event and audience, concise, attention-getting	Chairs Instrument Metronome Microphones Musical Notation Paper Music Racks Paper Pencil Pitch Pipe Risers Speakers Stage or Other Space Vocal Arrangements
Location	• Proper acoustics, comfortably accommodates audience	
Instruments (optional)	• Appropriate to composition	
Score	• Corresponds with instrument and/or vocal arrangement, original	
Vocals/Lyrics (optional	• Clear, concise, audible, pleasant, appropriate for mood/theme	
Appearance	• Attractive, uniform, neat, appropriate to occasion, not distracting	

Product: Play

Definition: A literary work written for performance.

Title of the Expert: Playwright, Director/Producer, Dramatist, Actor/Actress

Types of Plays:

Adaptions	No Theatre
Alternative	One-Act Play
Chronicle	Pantomime
Classical	Passion
Comedy	Play Musical
Commedia Dellarte	Puppet Play
Dinner Theatre	Radio Play
Drama	Reader's Theater
Expressionist	Realistic
Farce	Sanskrit
Full Length	Shadow
Guerilla	Shakespearean
Improvisation	Skits
Interlude	Solo Performance
Kabuki	Stage
Melodrama	Staged Reading
Mime	Surrealistic
Miracle	Tableau Vivant
Monodrama	Television
Monologue	Theater
Musical	Tragedy
Mystery	Trilogy

Words to Know:

Act	Interpretation
Action	Lighting
Actor	Makeup
Actress	Manager
Antagonist	Mask
Apron	Masking
Arena Stage	Mezzanine
Audience	Midstage
Audition	Mise-en-Scene
Avant-Garde	Movement
Backdrop	Music

Background

Balcony

Beam Projectors

Blocking

Border

Box Office

Burlesque

Cast

Casting

Center Stage

Character

Climax

Closure

Composition

Conflict

Costume

Critic

Cue

Curtain

Cyclorama

Decor

Design

Dialogue

Dinner Theatre

Downstage

Dress Rehearsal

Drop

Ellipsoidal

Entrance

Epilogue

Exit

Extras

Focus

Footlights

Foreground

Foreshadowing

Fresnel Light

Gesture

Green Room

Hero

Impersonate

Intermission

Narration

Opening Night

Orchestra Pit

Outdoor Stage

Paradox

Playbill

Playwright

Plot

Production

Prompt Box

Prompter

Prop

Proscenium

Protagonist

Reflector Light

Rehearsal

Rising Action

Run-Through

Satire

Scenario

Scene

Scenery

Script

Set

Signals

Sound Effects

Spotlight

Stage

Stage Direction

Stage Left

Stage Right

Strip Lights

Subscription

Suspense

Theater

Theme

Thrust

Trap Door

Trestle Stage

Upstage

Wardrobe

Wings

Helpful Hints:

- Determine your goals and priorities.
- Select the appropriate script for the audience.
- Experiment with different ways to say dialogue, move on stage, and handle props.
- Choose sets that enhance the production.
- Music should be used to create mood.
- Costumes should be authentic.
- The stage should have a dominant focal point.
- A prompter must be at every rehearsal.
- Publicize the performance.
- Always hold a dress rehearsal.
- If you do not have enough people for your play, have an actor play two parts.
- Attend plays in your community to generate ideas.
- Assemble your cast early on opening night.
- Rehearse, rehearse, rehearse!

Exemplary Producers:

Aristophanes	John Heywood
Aeschylus	Langston Hughes
George Abbot	Henrik Ibsen
Maxwell Anderson	William Inge
Maya Angelou	Henry Irving
André Antoine	Louis Jouvet
James Baldwin	George S. Kaufman
James M. Barrie	Elia Kazan
Samuel Beckett	George Kelly
Aphra Behn	Joan Littlewood
Thomas Betterton	Judith Malina
Bertolt Brecht	Vsevolod Meyerhold
Anton Chekhov	Arthur Miller
Agatha Christie	Jonathan Miller
Colley Cibber	Sean O'Casey
Marcus Cook Connerly	Clifford Odets
Gordon Craig	Joseph Papp
Rachel Crothers	Elmer Rice
Augustin Daly	Nicholas Rowe
William Dunlap	Frederich von Schiller
Marguerite Duras	William Shakespeare
José Echegaray	Bernard Shaw
Edna Ferber	Sam Shephard
Dario Fo	Wole Soyinka
Athol Fugard	Konstantin Stanislasky

Sir John Gielgud
W. S. Gilbert
J. W. Goethe
Lady Augusta Gregory
Peter Hall
Peter Handke
Lorraine Hansberry
Lillian Hellman
Beth Henley

Richard Steele
Peter Stein
August Strindberg
John Millington Synge
Thornton Wilde
Tennessee Williams
August Wilson
William Butler Yeats

Community Resources: Drama Teacher, Community Theater Director, English Teacher, Art Teacher

Quotes to Inspire:

"All the world's a stage."

—William Shakespeare

"Imagination, industry, and intelligence—'the three I's'—are all indispensable to the actress, but of these three the greatest is, without doubt, imagination."

—Ellen Terry

"All in all, creative act is not performed by the artist alone; the spectator brings the work in contact with the external world by deciphering and interpreting its inner qualifications and thus adds his contribution to the creative act. This becomes even more obvious when posterity gives its final verdict and sometimes rehabilitates forgotten artists."

—Marchal Duchamp

"The audience is the most revered member of the theater.
Without an audience there is no theater. Every technique learned by the actor, every curtain, every flat on the stage, every careful analysis by the director, every coordinated scene, is for the enjoyment of the audience. They are our guests, our evaluators, and the last spoke in the wheel which can then begin to roll.
They make the performance meaningful."

—Viola Spolin

"The stage is not merely the meeting place of all the arts, but is also the return of art to life."

—Oscar Wilde

"You need three things in the theatre—
the play, the actors, and the audience,
and each must give something."

—Kenneth Haigh

Product Criteria Grid

Product: Play

Components	Characteristics	Basic Materials
Title	• Representative of theme/content, correct spelling/grammar, captures attention	Accommodations for Audience Computer Costumes Cue Cards Lights Paper Pencil Props Stage
Script	• Appropriate for intended audience, interesting and relevant dialogue, characters and/or narration descriptive stage directions	
Actors	• Audible clear voice, suitable and accurate use of dialect, natural and realistic movement and gestures, expressive, accurate portrayal of character	
Set	• Realistic, representative of time period and location, aesthetically appealing, interesting, well-lit	
Costumes	• Authentic to time period, well-fitted, durable, attractive	

Product: Puppet Show

Definition: A story brought to life through the manipulation of puppets, movement, and voice.

Title of Expert: Puppeteer

Types of Puppets:

Fantoccini	Paper Bag
Finger	Push
Glove	Rod
Hand	Shadow
Handkerchief	Sock
Marionette	Spoon
Mouth	Tube

Words to Know:

Audience	Music
Banraku	Plasticine
Character	Props
Curtain	Rehearsal
Dowel	Scenery
Felt	Script
Footlights	Sound Effects
Manipulate	Stage
Movement	Voice

Helpful Hints:

- If there is more than one puppeteer, work out backstage positioning according to where you want each puppet to appear on stage.
- Keep puppets straight; they have a tendency to droop when your hand grows tired.
- Keep puppet's height constant.
- Make sure puppets face one another when talking to each other.
- Speak clearly and distinctly.
- Make sure the puppet's appearance and voice suit its part.
- The face of a puppet will always look the same; you must express its emotions using other methods.
- Make the puppet's costume long enough to cover your arm from view.
- Use props to develop the story, but keep them simple and use them only when necessary.
- Music is best used before a show starts to set a mood or atmosphere.
- Select plays to delight you and your audience.
- Design your stage to suit you and your budget.
- A table turned on its side, a sheet hanging from a doorway, and a broom suspended from

two chairs with a sheet draped over the broom can all serve as a stage.
- Try to make movements and voices distinctive for each puppet.

Exemplary Producers:

Bill Barretta	Sherri Lewis
Edgar Bergen	Laurent Mourquet
Keven Clash	Jerry Nelson
Jim Henson	Frank Oz
Sid and Marty Krofft	Steve Whitmire

Community Resources: Puppetry Guild, Librarian, Community Theater, Early Childhood Teachers

Quote to Inspire:

"Come children, let us shut up the box and the puppets, for our play is played out."
—William Makepeace Thakerey

Product Criteria Grid

Product: Play

Components	Characteristics	Basic Materials
Title	• Representative of topic/theme, appealing, creative	Buttons Computer Construction Paper Fabric Hammer Paint Pipe Cleaners Scissors Stage Wooden Dowels
Theme	• Appropriate for intended audience, relates to topic	
Puppets	• Large enough to be seen by audience, representative of character being depicted, durable, easy to manipulate, original	
Script	• Appropriate for intended audience, interesting dialogue	
Voice	• Representative of character; audible, appropriate volume, tone, and pitch; enhances character's emotions/feelings	
Stage	• Properly conceals puppeteers, sturdy, backdrop complements puppets	

Product: Simulation

Definition: An interactive activity composed of elements that portray an accurate representation or model of some external reality.

Title of Expert: Simulator, Game Designer

Types of Simulations:

Action Mazes	Free Form Role
Assigned Role	Function Game
Case Study	Limited Role
Computerized	Stochastic Game
Crisis Game	

Words to Know:

Adaptation	Participation
Algorithm	Planning
Choices	Priority
Communication	Probability
Competition	Problem Solving
Compromise	Prototype
Conflict	Purpose
Consequences	Qualitative
Cooperation	Quantitative
Decision Making	Reality
Delegation	Resources
Evaluation	Role-Playing
Fantasy	Rules
Models	Scenario
Negotiation	Society
Objectives	Solution
Options	

Helpful Hints:

- Clearly define the problem area to be simulated.
- Identify the roles within the simulation and limit play to a select group of characters.
- Don't forget to state the resources that are available.
- Remember, proper research will make your simulation more realistic.
- Write well-stated, clear rules that include things that can and cannot be done.
- Do not make the game too complicated. Start with a few rules and develop more if necessary.

- Schedule an evaluation period at the end. This will give you ideas to improve your simulation.
- Try the simulation out on a few friends. Record problems that are encountered and develop solutions.
- Remember that individuals who have participated in your simulation are your best critics.

Exemplary Producers:

Clark Abt	Paul Twelker
Robert Horn	John Washburn
Ray Glazier	David Zuckerman

Community Resources: Business Strategist, Computer Game Designer, Military Strategist, Pilot, Teacher of the Gifted

Quotes to Inspire:

"The very definition of the real becomes:
that of which it is possible to give an equivalent reproduction …
The real is not only what can be reproduced,
but that which is always already reproduced.
The hyperreal."

—Jean Baudrillard

"Fantasies are more than substitutes for unpleasant reality;
they are also dress rehearsals, plans.
All acts performed in the world begin in the imagination."

—Barbara Grizzuti Harrison

"Reality leaves a lot to the imagination."

—John Lennon

Product Criteria Grid

Product: Simulation

Components	Characteristics	Basic Materials
Title	• Relevant to topic/concept, captures interest, original	Computer Costumes Paper Pencil Props Resource Books
Theme/Concept	• Relevant to topic, appropriate for intended audience, nonlinear, allows for decision making	
Purpose/Goal	• Cleary stated, significant to theme	
Rules	• Clear, concise, precise, easy to understand	
Roles	• Relevant to purpose, well-defined	
Props	• Durable, enhances simulation	
Conclusion	• Re-examines key concepts	

Performance Resources

Dance

Books

Castle, K. (1996). *Ballet.* New York: Kingfisher Books.

Grau, A. (1998). *Dance.* New York: Knopf.

Jones, B. T. (1998). *Dance.* New York: Hyperion Press.

Levien, J. (1995). *Duncan dance: A guide for young people ages six to sixteen.* Pennington, NJ: Princeton Book Company Publications.

Medova, M. (1997). *Ballet for beginners.* Northampton, MA: Sterling Publications.

Prior, N. J. (1997). *Dance crazy: Star turns from ballet to belly dancing (True stories).* New York: Allen & Unwin.

Thomas, A. (1987). *Ballet: An Usborne guide.* Tulsa, OK: EDC Publications.

Web sites

http://www.ens-lyon.fr/~esouche/danse/dance.html
Dance Pages

http://www.danceonline.com
Dancing on a Line

Experiment

Books

Bleifeld, M. (1997). *Adventures with biology: Biology experiments for young people (Adventures with science).* Springfield, NJ: Enslow Publishers.

Churchill, E. R. (1997). *Amazing science experiments with everyday materials.* Northampton, MA: Sterling Publications.

DiSpezio, M. A. (1998). *Awesome experiments in electricity & magnetism.* Northampton, MA: Sterling Publications.

DiSpezio, M. A. (1998). *Awesome experiments in force & motion.* Northampton, MA: Sterling Publications.

Glover, D. M. (1995). *Batteries, bulbs, and wires: Science facts and experiments (Young discoverers)*. New York: Kingfisher Books.

Web sites

http://www.sciserv.org/teacher/scimeth.htm
The Scientific Method

http://users.massed.net/~wphillip/scimeth7.htm
Scimethod

http://www.suffolk.lib.ny.us/youth/jcsexperiments.html
Just Curious—Science Experiments

Monologue

Books

Evans, C., & Smith, L. (1992). *Acting and theatre*. Tulsa, OK: EDC Publications.

Gaffigan, C. (1994). *By kids, for kids: A collection of original monologues for kids and teenagers 6 to 18 years old*. New York: Excalibur Publishing.

Kehert, P. (1990). *Winning monologues for young actors: 65 honest-to-life characterizations to delight young actors and audiences of all ages*. Colorado Springs, CO: Meriwether Publishing.

Muir, K. (Ed.). (1995). *Childsplay: A collection of scenes and monologues for children*. New York: Limelight Editions.

Slaight, C., & Sharrar, J. (1995). *Multicultural monologues for young actors*. Lyme, NH: Smith & Kraus.

Web site

http://www.execpc.com/~blankda/monologbooks.html
Monologue Books

Musical Performance

Books

Ardley, N. (1989). *Music (Eyewitness books)*. New York: Knopf.

Ardley, N. (1995). *Young person's guide to music*. New York: Dorling Kindersley Publishing.

Brown, R. J. (1994). *How to play saxophone.* New York: St. Martin's Press.

Powell, S. (1995). *Hit me with music: How to start, manage, record, and perform with your own rock band.* Brookfield, CT: Millbrook Press.

Provost, R. (1997). *The art and technique of performance.* New York: Music Sales Corp.

Toff, N. (1996). *The flute book: A complete guide for students and performers.* New York: Oxford University Press.

Wilson, C. (1996). *The Kingfisher young people's book of music.* New York: Kingfisher Books.

Software

Magicbaton Jr. Kids Ages 3–8 Can Conduct Their Own Virtual Concerts!!
Edirol Corporation North America
808 Harrison Ave. Ste. 2010
P.O. Box 4919
Blaine, WA 98231-4919
Phone: (800) 380-2580

MiBAC Music Software
P.O. Box 468
Northfield, MN 55057
Phone: (800) 645-3945
Internet: http://www.mibac.com • E-mail: info@mibac.com

Web sites

http://www.childrensmusic.org/index.html
Children's Music Web

http://www.unm.edu/~loritaf/pnokids.html#music
The Piano Education Page—Just for Kids

http://hukilau.com/kidsrule/dbkids/instruments.html
Kids Rule! Music Instruments

Play

Books

Bany-Winters, L. (1997). *On stage: Theater games and activities for kids.* Chicago: Chicago Review.

Bentley, N., & Guthrie, D. (1996). *Putting on a play: The young playwright's guide to scripting, directing, and performing.* Brookfield, CT: Millbrook Press.

Bolton, R. (1998). *Showtime!: Over 75 ways to put on a show.* New York: DK Publishing.

Bulloch, I., & James, D. (1996). *An actor (I want to be series).* Chicago: World Book.

Gerke, P. (1996). *Multicultural plays for children: Grades 4–6.* Lyme, NH: Smith & Kraus.

Novelly, M. C. (1985). *Theatre games for young performers.* Colorado Springs, CO: Meriwether Publications.

Rooyackers, P. (1997). *101 Drama games for children: Fun and learning with acting and make-believe.* Cedar Rapids, IA: Hunter House.

Thistle, L. (1997). *Dramatizing myths and tales: Creating simple plays.* White Plains, NJ: Dale Seymour Publications.

Software

Opening Night
MECC
6160 Summit Drive North
Minneapolis, MN 55430-4003
Phone: (612) 569-1500
Internet: http://www.mecc.com

Web sites

http://www.stagekids.com
Stage Kids The Edu-Tainment Company

http://www.miranda.force9.co.uk/infoweb/index.html
Info Web—Preparing your Production

Puppet Show

Books

Engler, L. (1997). *Making puppets come alive: How to learn and teach hand puppetry.* New York: Dover Publications.

Fling, H. (1973). *Marionettes: How to make and work them.* New York: Dover Publications.

Fortney, A. J. (1983). *Puppets: Methods and materials.* Worcester, MA: Davis Publications.

Lade, R. (1996). *The most excellent book of how to be a puppeteer.* Brookfield, CT: Copper Beech Books.

Long, T. C. (1995). *Make your own performing puppets.* New York: Sterling Publications.

Ross, L. (1990). *Hand puppets: How to make and use them.* New York: Dover Publications.

Web sites

http://www.puppet.org/education.html
Center for Puppetry Arts Education Programs

http://www.puppeteers.org/guilds/default.htm
Puppetry Guilds Associated with Puppeteers of America

Simulation

Books

Abt, C. (1987). *Serious games.* Lanham, MD: University Press of America.

Gredler, M. (1994). *Designing and evaluating games and simulations: A process approach.* Houston, TX: Gulf Publishing.

Jones, K. (1997). *Icebreakers: A sourcebook of games, exercises, and simulations.* Houston, TX: Gulf Publishing.

Software

SimTown
Maxis, Inc.
2 Theatre Square
Orinda, CA 94563-3346
Phone: (510) 254-9700

Web sites

http://vanessa.www.media.mit.edu/people/vanessa/part-sims/index.html
Participatory Simulations

http://www.interact-simulations.com
Interaction Publishers, Inc.

CHAPTER VII

Written Products

Products that record ideas and knowledge through writing and composition fall within this category. Written products include but are not limited to:

Activity Sheet	Journal
Biography	Letters
Book	Newspaper Article
Checklist	Poems
Classified Advertisement	Questionnaire
Critique	Report
Description	Research Paper
Diary	Script
Dictionary	Song
Editorial	Story
Essays	Test
Glossary	

Included in this chapter are the profiles of 11 types of written products. The definitions, titles of experts, types, words to know, helpful hints, exemplary producers, community resources, and quotes to inspire for each product are detailed. These listings should be expanded as new information is uncovered during the research and product development process. Product grids that provide the components, characteristics, and basic materials necessary are also given, as well as authentic examples of written products created by students. A bibliography of books, web sites, and software specific to written products is included at the end of the chapter for future reference.

Product: Biography

Definition: A literary form that conveys the history or record of a person's life.

Title of Expert: Biographer

Types of Biography:

Campaign	Reductive
Historical	Scholarly
Literary	Scientific
Political	Spiritual
Psychological	Unauthorized

Words to Know:

Authenticity	Interview
Bias	Investigation
Bibliography	Letters
Character	Library Research
Chronology	Narrative
Documents	Newspapers
Evidence	Objectivity
Fact	Outline
Fiction	Personal
Footnotes	Primary Sources
Genre	Quotations
Hagiography	Realism
Information	Records
Interpretation	Secondary Sources

Helpful Hints:

- Select someone whom you can learn about and for whom there is reliable information available.
- Interview the person if possible.
- Be as unbiased as possible.
- Check your facts and figures.
- Do not use hearsay, only reliable sources.
- Write objectively.
- Make certain all-important details are included.
- Read several biographies and analyze their style before starting your writing.

Exemplary Producers:

Ray Stannard Baker
James Boswell
Fawn M. Brodie
Jean Fritz
James Anthony Froude
Frank Harris
William Henry Herndon
William Dean Howells
Ernest Jones
Sir Sidney Lee

Thomas Moore
John Morley
Allan Nevins
John George Nicolay
Sir Harold Nicholson
James Parton
Plutarch
Robert Southey
Lytton Strachey

Community Resources: College Professors, English Teachers, Historians, Librarians, Writers

Quotes to Inspire:

"Biography is a very definite region bounded on the north by history,
on the south by fiction, on the east by obituary, and on the west by tedium."
—Philip Guedalla

"The secret of biography resides in finding the link between talent and achievement.
A biography seems irrelevant if it doesn't discover the overlap
between what the individual did and the life that made this possible.
Without discovering that, you have shapeless happenings and gossip."
—Leon Edel

"Biography is to give a man some kind of shape after his death."
—Virginia Woolf

"A biographer is an artist upon oath."
—Sir Desmond MacCarthy

"A well-written life is almost as rare as a well-spent one."
—Thomas Carlyle

Product Criteria Grid

Product: Biography

Components	Characteristics	Basic Materials
Title	• Captures reader's attention, original, related to the topic	Almanac Computer Paper Pencil Pens Personal Documents Resource Books Tape Recorder Thesaurus
Person/Character	• Notable, of interest/appeal, described in depth	
Information/Facts	• Accurate, depicting of character's traits, significant, nonbiased, well-supported	
Sources	• Reliable, nonbiased, appropriately referenced	
Mechanics	• Appropriate choice of words, correct spelling/grammar, complete reference given for quotations/sources	
Organization	• Meaningful; has incidents, descriptions, and significance throughout; uniform	

Product: Book

Definition: A set of written, printed, or blank pages fastened along one side and encased between protective covers.

Title of Expert: Author, Editor, Publisher

Types of Books:

Anthology	Medical
Adventure	Memoirs
Alphabet	Mystery
Autobiography	Non-Fiction
Biography	Novel
Classics	Picture
Cookbook	Pop-Up
Directory	Reference
Fiction	Scientific
Guide	Short Stories
Historical	Sports
How-To	Textbook
Humorous	Travel
Manual	Wordless

Words to Know:

Acknowledgments	Introduction
Agent	Jacket/Cover
Appendix	Layout
Author	Literature
Best-Seller	Manuscript
Bibliography	Paperback
Bound	Plot
Chapter	Preface
Characters	Prose
Composition	Prospectus
Copyright	Publication Date
Dedication	Query
Design	Resource List
Editing	Revision
Edition	Royalty
Editor	Sequel
Figure	Setting
Footnotes	Submission

Genre	Summary
Glossary	Table of Contents
Hardback	Title
Illustration	Topic
Index	Volume

Helpful Hints:

- Designate a time and place to write.
- Spend time in bookstores and libraries.
- Read a lot of books.
- Write everyday.
- Set a deadline for completion.
- Have writing tools handy (pencil, paper, computer, thesaurus, dictionary, style guide, etc.).
- If composing on the computer, use the spell check!
- Omit unnecessary or meaningless words.
- Know your audience.
- Make writing clear, succinct, and organized.

Exemplary Producers:

Maya Angelou	Stephen King
Warren Bennis	Barbara Kingsolver
Judy Blume	Charles Kuralt
Jack Canfield	Sinclair Lewis
Eric Carle	Lois Lowry
Jimmy Carter	Toni Morrison
Julia Childs	Ayn Rand
Tom Clancy	Danielle Steele
Beverly Cleary	Mark Twain
William Faulkner	Chris Van Allsburg
Jean Fritz	Eudora Welty
John Grisham	Walt Whitman

Community Resources: Authors, Editors, English Teachers, Librarians, Literary Critics, Publisher

Quotes to Inspire:

"Books are for nothing, but to inspire."

—Ralph Waldo Emerson

"Read the best books first,
or you may not have a chance to read them at all."

—Henry David Thoreau

"Some books are to be tasted, others to be swallowed,
and some few to be chewed and digested."

—Francis Bacon

"The best time for planning a book is while you're doing the dishes."

—Agatha Christie

"The worth of a book is to be measured by what you can carry away from it."

—James Bryce

Latin Book

by Nicholas Sheldon Jones

Nicholas Sheldon Jones is a nine-year-old student attending fourth grade at Elmhurst Elementary in Ventura, CA. He enjoys playing soccer, drawing, and reading about history, and he plans to be a biochemist.

My idea for this project started when playing a game with my grandpa, Ron Sheldon. I missed a question that had to do with vocabulary, and my grandpa said that having knowledge of Latin would help with this type of question. This inspired me to learn Latin. Also, by learning this language, it might be easier to learn others, such as French, Italian, and Spanish.

I decided to make a children's book in Latin so that other children could be exposed to Latin, thus helping them have a better understanding of the roots of English words. Many product ideas came to mind, including the thought of writing a biography on Julius Caesar, but that seemed too overwhelming. Another idea was to write about the life of a boy in Rome. My dad helped to make this topic more specific, so I decided to compose a story about a slave in ancient Rome.

Next came the challenge of learning Latin. Our first thought was to find a class at the college, or a private teacher. There were none to be found. We did locate someone who could tutor in Latin, but they charged $25 for a half-hour, which was too expensive. Furthermore, the CD-ROM on learning Latin did not run on our computer. The final decision was to buy books on learning Latin and do it ourselves. With the assistance of my dad, I went through lessons in the books each evening. To organize my notes, a notebook was divided up into categories like verbs, nouns, and so forth. As new words were learned, they were written under the corresponding category. I also learned vocabulary, punctuation, and accusative and nominative cases in Latin. It was exciting to see what English words were derived from Latin, and the similarities of the two languages.

Now the book was ready to be written! After the storyline was decided, it was recorded on a piece of paper in English and then translated into Latin under each phrase. It was necessary to make the phrases simple so young children could understand them. Because I cannot draw people very well, photographs were selected to illustrate the story. My older friend played the role of Julius, the wealthy merchant, and I played Cincmatus, the slave. We both dressed in togas and turned the backyard into ancient Rome. Care was taken not to get the houses, swing sets, or telephone wires in the pictures to ensure authenticity. After taking many pictures, the best ones were selected and sent to my Uncle Peter. He scanned the photos into his computer, set the words, and laid out the pages for the book. From this, color copies of the pages were printed and then bound into a book.

This project taught me a lot. My understanding about the parts of a sentence and the forms of nouns, verbs, and so forth, was expanded, as well as my knowledge of how words in the English language originated. In addition, it was amazing to learn how complicated and expensive it is to produce a simple book. Furthermore, it took dedication to keep learning and reviewing Latin. My advice to children is to learn Latin, because it will help them learn other foreign languages. Remember what Winston Churchill once said: "If I ruled the world, I would let the clever ones learn Latin, and Greek for a treat."

A sample page from the Latin Book showing Julius, the wealthy merchant (left) and Cincmatus, the slave (right), as portrayed by an older friend (left) and Nicholas (right).

Product Criteria Grid

Product: Book

Components	Characteristics	Basic Materials
Title	• Attention-getting, concise, reflects content	Camera Computer Dictionary Glue Markers Paper Pencil Resource Books Ruler Scissors Style Guide Thesaurus Word Processing Software
Cover	• Aesthetically appealing, corresponds with content, neat	
Table of Contents (optional)	• Accurate, easy to use, proper location	
Content	• Of interest to intended audience, accurate, up to date, correct spelling and grammar	
Graphics (optional)	• Clear, corresponds with content, enhancing, appropriate size	
Layout	• Attractive, neat, logically organized	
Index (optional)	• Proper placement, accurate, comprehensive	
Credits	• All-inclusive, prominently displayed, accurate titles and recognition of responsibilities	
References	• Accurate, up to date, correct citation	

Product: Editorial

Definition: A journalistic or narrative essay that attempts to inform or explain, to persuade or convince, or to stimulate insight.

Title of the Expert: Editorial Writer, Editor, Editorialist

Types of Editorials:

Commentary	Humorous
Definitional	Newspaper
Endorsing	Persuasive
Entertaining	Problem Solving
Explanation	Radio
Historical	Television

Words to Know:

Advocacy	Details
Audience	Endorsement
Body	Ethics
Column	Issues
Conclusion	Opening
Controversy	Persuasion
Criticism	Rationale
Debate	Solution
Defense	Stance

Helpful Hints:

- Refer to significant news in a timely fashion.
- Select an issue the reader can relate to or is of local interest.
- Begin by getting the reader's attention, next persuade the reader, and finally prompt the reader to action.
- Always let several people proofread the editorial before it is published.
- Research carefully so that all your facts are accurate.
- In writing, keep command of your emotions.
- Read the newspaper editorial section.

Exemplary Producers:

James Gordon Bennett	Warren Lerude
John Bigelow	Roger B. Linscott
William Cullen Bryant	Walter Lippman

Hodding Carter
Philip Freneau
Philip L. Geyelin
E. L. Godkin
Henry Grady
Katherine Graham
Horace Greeley
Nelson Alexander Hamilton
William Randolph Hearst
Philip Kerby

Elijah Lovejoy
John Daniell Maurice
Joseph Pulitzer
Henry Raymond
William Rockhill
William Safire
F. Gilman Spencer
William Allen White
Walt Whitman

Community Resources: Journalist, Newspaper Writers, English Teacher, Professor of Journalism

Quotes to Inspire:

"An editor is someone who separates the wheat from the chaff and then prints the chaff."

—Adlai Stevenson

"I always write a good first line, but I have trouble in writing the others."

—Moliere

Product Criteria Grid

Product: Editorial

Components	Characteristics	Basic Materials
Title	• Concise, representative of issues presented, captures reader's attention	Computer Dictionary Paper Pencil Style Guide Thesaurus
Issue	• Relevant, timely, significant to intended audience, thoroughly discussed	
Body	• Clear, concise, well-written, engages reader, flows	
Mechanics	• Proper spelling and grammar	
Organization	• Logical sequence of information, paragraphs flow together	

Product: Essay

Definition: A short piece of nonfiction writing consisting of paragraphs about an idea based on an author's opinion.

Title of the Expert: Essayist, Writer, Author

Types of Essays:

Critical	Persuasive
Formal	Photo
Historical	Political
Humorous	Satirical
Informal	Scientific
Personal Narrative	Social

Words to Know:

Allusion	Passive Voice
Antonym	Person
Argument	Personal
Body	Persuasion
Composition	Point of View
Conclusion	Proofread
Content	Pros and Cons
Dialogue	Punctuation
Expression	References
Facts	Rough Draft
Generalization	Sentence
Insight	Simile
Introduction	Statement
Irony	Style
Main Points	Supporting Paragraphs
Mechanics	Synonym
Metaphor	Theme
Narrator	Thesis
Opinion	Title
Outline	Topic
Paragraph	Transition
Parallel	Verb tense

Helpful Hints:

- Be sure to check mechanics such as spelling, capitalization, punctuation, run-on sentences, fragments, and subject-verb agreement.
- Use readability level appropriate for intended audience.
- Do not use first person unless writing a personal narrative.
- Use a thesaurus to find the right word.
- Everything in the essay should support the thesis statement.
- The thesis statement should be in the introductory paragraph.
- Make sure you know enough about your selected subject to arrive at some kind of opinion.
- Think before you write.
- Consider both points that are in favor of and against your thesis.
- Write your thesis on a note card and put it on the wall in front of your desk. Keep it in view all the time you are working on your essay.
- Read to build your vocabulary.
- Save your best argument for last.
- Devote at least one full paragraph to every major pro argument in your full thesis statement.
- Have an "editor" proofread each draft.

Exemplary Producers:

Joseph Addison	John Locke
Matthew Arnold	John Stuart Mill
Sir Francis Bacon	Michel de Montaigne
James Baldwin	George Orwell
John Burroughs	Walter Pater
Joseph Brodsky	Alexander Pope
Willa Cather	Ezra Pound
John Jay Chapman	Agnes Repplier
Leon Daudet	George Bernard Shaw
Clarence Shepard Day	Susan Sontag
Joan Didion	Richard Steele
John Dryden	Robert Louis Stevenson
T. S. Eliot	Lionel Trilling
Ralph Waldo Emerson	Mark Twain
William Hazlitt	Robert Penn Warren
Aldous Huxley	Alice Walker
Charles Lamb	E. B. White
Jean Margaret Laurence	Virginia Woolf

Community Resources: English Teacher, Essayist, Journalist

Quotes to Inspire:

"Good writing connects one person's life experiences
to the lives of many others."

—Alice Walker

"A personal essay often states the writer's deepest beliefs."

—James Baldwin

"Essays reflect personal opinion
as well as objective reality."

—Joan Didion

"An essayist is a lucky person
who has found a way to discourse
without being interrupted."

—Charles Poore

Product Criteria Grid

Product: Essay

Components	Characteristics	Basic Materials
Title	• Relevant to theme, captures reader's attention	Computer Dictionary Note Cards Paper Pencil Style Guide Thesaurus
Theme	• Significant, relevant to audience, related to topic	
Introduction	• Captures reader's attention, states the thesis	
Argument	• Supported, consideration given to both sides	
Mechanics	• Correct spelling and grammar, logically organized	
Conclusion	• Summarizes main points, leaves reader satisfied	

Product: Magazine

Definition: A periodical containing a collection of articles, stories, pictures, or other features.

Title of Expert: Editor, Writer, Journalist

Types of Magazine Articles:

Consumer
Factual
Fictional
How-To
Human Interest
Humorous
Inspirational

Interview
Personal
Experience
Review
Self-Help
Sports
Travel

Words to Know:

Action Lead
Advertisement
Anecdotes
Anecdotal Lead
Annual
Article
Audience
Body
Center Spread
Characterization
Circulation
Conclusion
Content
Cover
Coverage
Cover Story
Description
Dialogue
Ending
Expository Lead
Feature
Free-Lance
Gazette

Glossy
Journal
Lead
Libel
Market
Monthly
Periodical
Persuasive
Publication
Quarterly
Query
Quote
Recap
Reference
Rejection
Research
Serial
Solicit
Source
Subject
Submission
Summary
Weekly

Helpful Hints:

- Make time for your writing.
- Choose a subject that will appeal to many readers.
- Use the title of the article to attract attention.
- Engage a reader's attention at the start and hold it until the end.
- Remember that rewriting is essential.
- Listen to what you have written.
- Alternate long and short sentences.
- Cover a lot of ground in the least possible number of words.
- Always note your sources in case facts are challenged.
- Direct quotes must be accurately attributed.
- Convey a sense of completion at the end so the reader is left satisfied.
- A factual article should be based on careful research.
- Keep basic reference books on hand, for example, a dictionary, thesaurus, book of quotations, style manual, and writer's handbook.
- Query letters must be as lively and well-written as the article you want to sell.

Exemplary Producers:

Charles Alexander
Margaret Caroline Anderson
Walter H. Annenberg
Samuel C. Atkinson
Edward William Bok
Margaret Bourke-White
Norman Cousins
Cyrus Kotzschmar Curtis
Charles Dickens
Marshall Field, III
B. C. Forbes
Arnold Gingrich
Gilbert Hovey Grosvenor
Sarah Josepha Buell Hale
William Randolph Hearst
John Harold Johnson
John F. Kennedy, Jr.

Henry Luce
Edward Sanford Martin
Thomas John Cardel Martyn
Rupert Murdoch
Conde Naste
Samuel Irving Newhouse
Edwin Newman
Harold Wallace Ross
William Shawn
Elizabeth Cady Stanton
Lincoln Steffens
Gloria Steinem
William M. Thackeray
James Grover Thurber
Dewitt Wallace
Jann Wenner

Community Resources: Editors, English Teachers/Professors, Journalists, Writers Conferences/Workshops

Quote to Inspire:

"A magazine or a newspaper is a shop.
Each is an experiment and represents a new focus,
a new ratio between commerce and intellect."

—John Jay Chapman

Product Criteria Grid

Product: Magazine

Components	Characteristics	Basic Materials
Title	• Attention-grabbing, concise, reflects content, prominent	Book of Quotations Camera Computer Dictionary Film Glue Markers Paper Pencils Ruler Scissors Stencils Thesaurus Writer's Handbook
Cover	• Eye-catching, aesthetically appealing, neat, corresponds with theme/content	
Table of Contents	• Accurate, easy to use, sequential	
Content	• Relevant topic, appealing to intended audience, interesting, correct grammar and spelling	
Advertisements (optional)	• In good taste, appropriate to audience, visually attractive, informative	
Graphics	• Clear, correspond with content, enhancing	
Layout	• Attractive, eye-catching, neat, logically organized	
Credits	• All-inclusive, prominently displayed, correct spelling, accurate titles and recognition of responsibilities	

Product: Newspaper

Definition: A publication regularly printed and distributed, which contains news, opinions, advertisements, and other items of general interest.

Title of Expert: Journalist, Columnist, Writer, Editor, Photographer/Photojournalist, Publisher

Types of Newspapers:

Business	National
Community	Political
Daily	Sunday
Evening	Tabloid

Words to Know:

Advertisement	Leaflet
Associated Press	Letter to the Editor
Assignment	Libel
Banner	Local Edition
Body Copy	Masthead
Business	National
Cartoon	Opinion
Clarity	Obituary
Classified	Pictures
Comic	Press
Current Events	Press Conference
Cutlines	Privacy
Daily Edition	Privileged
Dateline	Information
Deadline	Prominence
Editing	Proofreading
Editorial	Proximity
Elements	Readability
Feature	Reporter
Filler	Sidebar
Flag	Sports
Headline	Stringer
Insert	Style
International	Supplement
Interviews	Syndicated
Issue	Time Lines
Journalism	UPI/AP/Knight-Ridder

| Late Edition | Wire Service |
| Lead | Yellow Journalism |

Helpful Hints:

- Write at the reading level for your audience.
- Obtain at least two sources for all information to protect your credibility.
- Experiment with different page layouts to find the best design.
- Remember that you are accountable to the public for the fairness and accuracy of news reports.
- Report news of interest to your audience.
- Make sure you have names and titles spelled correctly and they are accurate.
- Give appropriate reference to all quotes.
- Use a recording device and take notes during interviews.
- Keep a positive relationship with sources of information.
- Remember, libel and invasion of privacy are legal offenses, and people who feel that they have been libeled can sue.
- Read the newspaper and look at newspapers from around the U.S.

Exemplary Producers:

Russell Wayne Baker	Ben Hecht
James Gordon Bennett, Jr.	Elsa Maxwell
James Gordon Bennett, Sr.	Robert R. McCormick
James Alonzo Bishop	Edgar Allen Poe
Arthur Brisbane	Joseph Pullitzer
William F. Buckley	Ernie Pyle
Katharine Graham	Walter Wellesley Smith
Horace Greeley	Mark Twain
William Randolph Hearst	William Allen White

Community Resources: English Teacher, Journalism Professor, Newspaper Editor, Newspaper Reporter

Quotes to Inspire:

"The only security of all is in a free press."

—Thomas Jefferson

"A good newspaper, I suppose, is a nation talking to itself."

—Arthur Miller

Product Criteria Grid

Product: Newspaper

Components	Characteristics	Basic Materials
Name	• Corresponds with community/readership, concise, easy to remember	Camera Computer Markers Paper Pencil Photocopier Printer Printing Press Ruler Stencils
Headings	• Prominent, bold, concise, direct, legible, neat	
Text/Content	• Correct grammar and spelling, engaging, of interest/significance to readership, timely	
Sections	• Prominently titled, appropriate for readership, logically organized	
Photographs/Graphics	• Clear, correspond with text, not offensive, significant	
Advertisements	• Appropriate to intent of newspaper, products/services of interest to readership, attractive, concise	
Cartoon/Comics	• Varied, neat, appropriate to readership, implicit	

Product: Poem

Definition: A select group of words put together into a composition to express an experience, emotion, or thought through vivid imaginative language.

Title of the Expert: Poet

Types of Poems:

Acrostic
Ballad
Cento
Cinquain
Clerihew
Couplet
Diamante
Elegy
Epic
Epitaph
Free Verse

Haiku
Iambic
Limerick
Lyric
Narrative
Ode
Pentameter
Quatrain
Sonnet
Tanka
Triplets

Words to Know:

Alliteration
Assonance
Consonance
Euphony
Hyperbole
Imagery
Irony
Metaphor
Meter
Onomatopoeia
Paradox
Poet Laureate

Pseudonym
Pun
Refrain
Rhyme
Rhythm
Simile
Stanza
Structure
Symbolism
Syntax
Verse

Helpful Hints:

- Read many examples of poetry. It will assist you in your writing.
- Take note of powerful words and phrases within the poetry you read.
- Discuss your interpretations of poems with others.
- Read the poems you write out loud. This will give you a sense of the rhythm you've created.
- Make use of a thesaurus to find the best word for the image you are trying to convey.

- Keep a portfolio of your poems.
- Try to express your experience, emotion, or thought in "images."

Exemplary Producers:

Anna Akhmatova	Francis Scott Key
Maya Angelou	Rudyard Kipling
Elizabeth Bishop	Denise Levertou
Louise Bogan	Amy Lowell
William Blake	Edna St. Vincent Millay
Anne Bradstreet	John Milton
Gwendolyn Brooks	Marianne Moore
Elizabeth Barrett Browning	Ogden Nash
Robert Browning	Sylvia Plath
Geoffrey Chaucer	Nelly Sachs
Samuel Taylor Coleridge	Carl Sandburg
Countee Cullin	Anne Sexton
ee cummings	Dame Edith Sitwell
Emily Dickenson	Robert Louis Stevenson
Hilda Doolittle	Sara Teasdale
Rita Dove	Alfred Lord Tennyson
T. S. Eliot	Monta Van Duyn
Ralph Waldo Emerson	William Wadsworth
Robert Frost	Alice Walker
Louise Gluck	Phillis Wheatley
John Keats	Walt Whitman

Community Resources: English Teacher, Local Poets, Writer's Guild

Quotes to Inspire:

"The art of the poet is to make ordinary words deliver extraordinary messages"

—Robert Frost

"Only poetry inspires poetry."

—Ralph Waldo Emerson

"To read a poem is to hear it with our eyes;
to hear it is to see it with our ears."

—Octavio Paz

"One merit of poetry few persons will deny:
it says more in fewer words than prose."

—Voltaire

Product Criteria Grid

Product: Poem

Components	*Characteristics*	*Basic Materials*
Title	• Concise, relevant to topic or theme of poem	Computer Dictionary Paper Pencil Rhyming Dictionary Thesaurus
Verses	• Appropriately organized according to poem type, effectively arranged	
Words	• Carefully selected, descriptive, properly convey message/mood, proper spelling appropriate for intended audience	
Rhythm/Meter	• Consistent with poem type, corresponds with theme/topic, enhances poem	
Rhyme (optional)	• Enhances poem; natural, not forced	

Product: Scientific Report

Definition: A written paper describing original research results.

Title of the Expert: Researcher, Scientist

Types of Scientific Reports:

Dissertation	Monograph
Experimental	Thesis

Words to Know:

Abstract	Method
Analyze	Observation
Control	Procedure
Criteria	Reliability
Data	Research
Discussion	Results
Dissertation	Stimulus
Evaluate	Subjects
Evidence	Summarize
Experiment	Survey
Hypothesis	Synthesize
Inquiry	Test
Introduction	Theory
Investigator	Title
Laboratory	Validity
Materials	

Helpful Hints:

- Remember the acronym IMRAD, which stands for the components of a scientific report (Introduction, Methods, Results, and Discussion).
- The title should accurately describe the contents of the report, because improperly titled reports may never reach the intended audience.
- Be sure to defend your selected method over other available methods.
- Accurately identify all experimental animals, plants, micro-organisms, and so forth.
- If you use human subjects, thoroughly describe your criteria for selection.
- Use headings and subheadings appropriately.
- Be precise.
- State your conclusions as clearly as possible.
- Don't forget to end with a short summary regarding the significance of the work.
- Use tables to present repetitive data.

- Before submitting for publication, be sure to read instructions to authors for the journal for which you plan to submit.
- If data show pronounced trends, making a graph/table(s) is advised.

Exemplary Producers:

Roger Bacon	Sir Francis Galton
Niels Henrik David Bohr	Louis Leakey
Rachel Carson	Mary Leakey
Marie Curie	Abraham Maslow
Pierre Curie	Marie Goeppert Mayer
Sir Henry Hallett Dale	Barbara McClintock
John Dalton	Maria Mitchell
Charles Darwin	Sir Isaac Newton
Albert Einstein	Jean Piaget
Gertrude Belle Elion	Albert Bruce Sabin
Michael Faraday	Carl Sagan
Camille Flammarion	Jonas Salk
Alexander Fleming	Louis Terman
Sigmund Freud	Rosalyn Sussman Yalow

Community Resources: College Professors, Science Teachers, Graduate Reader/Dissertation Publishers

Quotes to Inspire:

"Without publication, science is dead."

—Gerard Piel

"Scientific inquiry requires investigators to challenge the validity and interpretation of evidence; hence the name research."

—Wayne G. Watson

"A tabular presentation of data is often the heart or, better, the brain, of a scientific paper."

—Peter Morgan

"In my writing I am acting as a mapmaker, an explorer of psychic areas ... a cosmonaut of inner space, and I see no point in exploring areas that have already been thoroughly surveyed."

—William Burroughs

Pond Life Book

by Julia C. Napolitano

Julia C. Napolitano is 10 years old and in the fifth grade at Rosendale Elementary School in Niskayuna, NY. She plays the violin and loves to draw, write, and read. Her ambition is to be a writer someday.

My teacher, Ms. Randee Hartz, and all the fifth-grade teachers in our state have been teaching their students about ponds and pond life. My class collected pond organisms and examined them under microscopes. It's really fun to study small things up close with the microscope. The assignment was to organize all the data, write, and illustrate a book of our own. Each student's book was unique and interesting. My book was entitled *Pond Critters*. It was planned through the careful use of calendars, deadlines, guidelines, and checklists. I typed the pages of my book and organized them in a three-ring binder. Pictures of tadpoles, scuds, crayfish, and everything in between were obtained from the computer and used in making my own illustrations with colored pencils and markers.

My book was evaluated using a rubric, which is a way of categorizing where your efforts rate in a certain area. The ratings ranged from 4, meaning "superior," 3 for "high quality," 2 for "fair," or 1, meaning "inferior." My book landed a 4! The grade was determined by such things as whether our visuals were neat and worked to enhance the content of the book.

This project incorporated both science and writing. Science, because scientific instruments such as microscopes and thermometers were used, and because we took the role of scientists to observe and study pond creatures. It also encompassed writing, because a book was written from the data collected. The pride from my work prompted me to share the completed book with many friends and family members.

Many skills and a lot of knowledge were gained while writing and putting the book together. Also, I now have the ability to carefully collect, look at, and release organisms, plus a real appreciation of ponds and their life forms. Some advice I would give to help others is: If and when you do a project or unit similar to this, remember that you should follow instructions, stay calm, and treat the organisms carefully and with respect. After all, they are alive, even if you can't see them! I also think people should remember that any project they do, whether it's a book they write or an illustration they draw, reflects who they are, and they should always be proud of anything they accomplish that shows positive effort. I highly recommend that, in a lifetime, each person should create something unique. Who knows, maybe you and your creation will become famous! My motto is give positive opportunities your best shot!

Product Criteria Grid

Product: Scientific Report

Components	*Characteristics*	*Basic Materials*
Title	• Representative of content/topic, concise	Calculator Computer Graphing Paper Pencil Ruler Statistical Software Packages Testing Instrument(s)
Content	• Significant, of interest to intended audience, timely, accurate	
Method	• Thoroughly described, appropriate, ethical, valid and reliable, sample appropriate to experiment	
Results	• Accurately derived, cleary stated, precise calculations, suitably summarized	
Tables (optional)	• Neat, logically organized, appropriately labeled, corresponds with text, presents relevant data	
Photographs/Figures	• Clear, corresponds with text, enhancing	
Conclusion	• Comprehensive, emphasis on key findings, recommendations for future study	
References	• Accurate, appropriately placed, comprehensive, correct citations	

Product: Script

Definition: The written text of a play, broadcast, or movie.

Title of the Expert: Playwright, Screenwriter

Types of Scripts:

Adaptation	Pantomine
Documentary	Play
Dramatic	Puppet
Full-Length	Radio
Improvisation	Reader's Theater
Monodrama	Skit
Monologue	Sound Story
Musical	Television

Words to Know:

Action	Narrator
Actor/Actress	Plot
Acts	Props
Antagonist	Protagonist
Audition	Rehearsal
Beat	Role
Cast	Scene
Characters	Scenery
Conflict	Setting
Crew	Situation
Dialogue	Sound Effects
Diction	Stage
Directions	Theme
Expression	Title
Gestures	Tour
Intermission	Understudy

Helpful Hints:

- One page of a script equals about one minute of time on stage.
- Describe the time and place for each scene.
- Stage directions are written in parentheses under the characters' names.
- Character names are typed in all capital letters.
- Select characters with whom the audience will identify.
- Jot down your ideas about potential characters in a notebook.

- Develop one conflict as the center of your script.
- The dialogue in the script must move the play forward.
- Collaborate with others to change and strengthen your work.

Exemplary Producers:

James Agee	Ayn Rand
Samuel N. Behrman	William Shakespeare
T. S. Eliot	George Bernard Shaw
Lillian Hellman	Sam Shephard
Langston Hughes	Neil Simon
George S. Kaufman	Thorton Wilder
Arthur Miller	Oscar Wilde
Eugene O'Neill	Tennessee Williams

Community Resources: Drama Teacher, English Teacher, Performing Arts Center, Community Theater Director, University Drama Department

Quotes to Inspire:

"A playwright ... is ... the litmus paper of the arts."

—Arthur Miller

"Man is least himself when he talks in his own person. Give him a mask, and he will tell you the truth."

—Oscar Wilde

Product Criteria Grid

Product: Script

Components	Characteristics	Basic Materials
Title	• Appropriate to topic, original	Computer
Plot	• Appropriate to topic and intended audience, interesting, original	Dictionary Paper Pencil
Setting	• Thoroughly described, relevant to plot and characters	Style Guide Thesaurus
Characters	• Thoroughly described, well-developed, interesting, appealing to intended audience	
Dialogue	• Accurately reflects character(s), engaging, enhances plot/theme, realistic	

Product: Short Story

Definition: A narrative producing an emotional impression by means of sustained emphasis on a single climatic incident or situation.

Title of the Expert: Writer

Types of Short Stories:

Conflict	Mystery
Decision	Novel
Discovery	Romance
Fantasy	Science
Historical	

Words to Know:

Action	Metaphor
Alliteration	Mood
Anecdote	Motive
Atmosphere	Narrations
Audience	Novellar
Beginnings	Pacing
Brainstorming	Persuasive
Cause and Effect	Plot
Characters	Point of View
Cliches	Polishing
Climate	Registration Slips
Climax	Revising
Conflict	Royalties
Descriptive	Scenes
Dialect	Simile
Dialogue	Situation
Editing	Stereotypes
Editions	Story Plan
Endings	Story Tension
Environment	Struggle
Events	Suspense
Fantasy	Theme
Feedback	Thesaurus
Figures of Speech	Tone
First Draft	Word Processor
Informative	

Helpful Hints:

- Select an interesting title to capture attention.
- The first step is to develop a story plan.
- Select a notebook and keep it with you at all times for recording new ideas.
- Good stories stand or fall on good characters.
- Select the right environment for your story.
- Keep a thesaurus, dictionary, and style guide on hand for quick reference.
- Use descriptive words to create vivid characters, setting, and imagery.

Exemplary Producers:

Maya Angelou	Thomas Mann
Ray Bradbury	Katherine Mansfield
Pearl S. Buck	Gabriel Garcia Marquez
Truman Capote	Herman Melville
Willa Cather	James Michener
Geoffrey Chaucer	Flannery O'Connor
Charles Waddell Chestnutt	John O'Hara
Charles Dickens	Joyce Carol Oates
Ellen Douglas	Dorothy Parker
F. Scott Fitzgerald	Katherine Anne Porter
Ellen Gilcrest	Gertrude Stein
Nathanial Hawthorne	Robert Louis Stevenson
Ernest Hemingway	Mark Twain
James Joyce	John Updike
Rudyard Kipling	Eudora Welty
Jason Lason	Edith Wharton
Sinclair Lewis	Virginia Woolf

Community Resources: Writers, English Teachers, Book Store Personnel

Quotes to Inspire:

"Style is something you develop over time, not something you can install like a computer."
—Ronald B. Tobias

"One of the greatest quirks of the human mind is the capacity for being moved to tears, laughter, anger, anxiety, joy by a 'person' who exists nowhere except in imagination! The explanation is identity."
—Jane Fitz-Randolph

"Novel—a short story padded."
—Ambrose Pierce

Product Criteria Grid

Product: Short Story

Components	Characteristics	Basic Materials
Title	• Stimulating, appealing, captures attention of the reader	Book of Quotes Computer Dictionary Paper Pencils Pens Style Guide Thesaurus
Plot	• Appropriate for intended audience, interesting, unique	
Beginning	• Captures the reader's attention, introduces the characters and setting	
Characters	• Thoroughly described considering physical aspects, activities, personal thoughts, feelings, attitudes, and personality; interesting; appealing to intended audience	
Setting	• Descriptive; appropriate for mood, characters, and plot of the story; accurate; realistic	
Middle	• Builds suspense, hold reader's attention, shows complication through action and dialogue	
Climax	• High point of suspense, demonstrates the turning point of the story	
Ending	• Satisfies the reader, demonstrates change in the main characters, memorable, ties up loose ends	

Product: Song

Definition: A piece of music, either vocal, instrumental, or both, combining melody, rhythm, harmony, and timbre.

Title of Expert: Composer, Lyricist, Songwriter

Types of Songs:

Alternative	Instrumental
Ballad	Jazz
Blues	Jingle
Calypso	Lullaby
Carol	Opera
Chant	Pop
Classical	Rap
Country	Rock 'n Roll
Folk	Serenade
Gospel	Vocal
Hymn	

Words to Know:

Accents	Modulation
Accidentals	Mood
Accompaniment	Movement
Articulation	Naturae
Atonality	Note
Bar	Octave
Bass	Orchestra
Bass Clef	Pattern
Beams	Percussion
Beat	Pitch
Binary	Polytonality
Brace	Quarter Note
Cadence	Quartet
Canon	Repetition
Chords	Rest
Climax	Rhythm
Composition	Scale
Conductor	Sharp
Copyright	Slur
Counterpoint	Solo
Demo	Sonata

Dissonance	Space
Dominant	Staccatissimo
Dots	Staccato
Flag	Staff
Flat	Staves
Fugue	Subdivisions
Glissando	Symphony
Half Note	Tenor
Harmony	Tenuto
Instruments	Texture
Interlude	Timbre
Key	Time Signatures
Key Signatures	Tone
Lead Sheet	Tonic
Lyric	Treble Clef
Major/Minor	Tres
Marcato	Unison
Melody	Whole Note
Meter	
Metronome	

Helpful Hints:

- Ideas for songs are all around you. Carry a notebook and record possible ideas.
- Decide whether you want to write lyrics, music, or both.
- Match the music to the lyrics. Decide on the feelings/mood that you want to convey.
- Don't let your music run too long. Most songs are about three and a half minutes in length.
- Collaborate with others … with a lyricist if you are a composer … with a composer if you are a lyricist.
- Record a demo.
- Select a strong title that sticks in the listener's mind.

Exemplary Producers:

Paul Anka	Madonna
Ludwig von Beethoven	Henry Mancini
Irving Berlin	Chuck Mangione
Keith Carradine	Paul McCartney
Ray Charles	Johnny Mercer
Eric Clapton	Joni Mitchell
Phil Collins	Wolfgang Mozart
Jim Croce	Roy Orbison
Christopher Cross	Cole Porter

Fats Domino
Bob Dylan
Stephen Foster
Aretha Franklin
George Gershwin
Ira Gershwin
Merle Haggard
Oscar Hammerstein
George Frederic Handel
W. C. Handy
Elton John
Carole King
Kris Kristofferson
John Lennon

Elvis Presley
Giacomo Puccini
Lionel Ritchie
Richard Rodgers
Franz Schubert
Gunther Schuller
Paul Simon
Bruce Springstein
Igor Stravinsky
Peter Tchaikovsky
Hank Williams
Paul Williams
Meredith Wilson
Stevie Wonder

Community Resource People: Local Musicians, Music Teacher, University Music Department

Quotes to Inspire:

"A nation creates music—the composer only arranges it."

—Mikhail Glinka

"In writing songs, I've learned as much from Cézanne as I have from Woody Guthrie."

—Bob Dylan

"It is the best of all trades, to make songs, and the second best to sing them."

—Hilaire Belloc

"There is nothing remarkable about it. All one has to do is hit the right keys at the right time and the instrument plays itself."

—Johann Sebastian Bach

"Music is the art of thinking with sounds."

—Jules Combarieu

Product Criteria Grid

Product: Song

Components	Characteristics	Basic Materials
Title	• Conveys message of song, short and concise, easy to remember	Instruments (optional) Metronome Musical Notation Paper Paper Pencils Pens Pitch Pipe Tape Recorder
Lyrics (optional)	• Communicate message through expressive language, set to a specific rhythm, thought-provoking	
Musical Notations	• Neat, legible, accurate	
Melody	• Appropriate for intended message, pleasing to the ear, catchy, original	

Written Resources

Biography

Books

O'Connor, U. (1997). *Biographers and the art of biography.* Boulder, CO: Irish American Book Co.

Parke, C. N. (1996). *Biography: Writing lives.* New York: Twayne Publishing.

Schwartz, T. (1990). *The complete guide to writing biographies.* Cincinnati, OH: Writer's Digest Books.

Web site

http://www.biography.com
Biography

Book

Books

Chapman, G. (1994). *Making books: A step-by step guide to your own publishing.* Brookfield, CT: Millbrook Press.

Christelow, E. (1997). *What do authors do?* New York: Clarion Books.

Edelstein, S. (1997). *1,818 ways to write better and get published.* Cincinnati, OH: Writers Digest Books.

Edelstein, S. (1993). *30 steps to becoming a writer and getting published: The complete starter kit for aspiring writers.* Cincinnati, OH: Writers Digest Books.

Fenimore, F. (1992). *The art of the handmade book: Designing, decorating, and binding.* Chicago: Chicago Review Press.

Guthrie, D., Bentley, N., & Arnsteen, K. K. (1994). *The young author's do-it-yourself book: How to write, illustrate, and produce your own book.* Brookfield, CT: Millbrook Press.

Larsen, M. (1997). *How to write a book proposal.* Cincinnati, OH: Writers Digest Books.

Page, S. (1997). *The shortest distance between you and a published book.* New York: Broadway Books.

Snell, M. (1997). *From book idea to bestseller: What you absolutely, positively must know to make your book a success.* Rocklin, CA: Prima Publishing.

Stevens, J. (1995). *From pictures to words: A book about making a book.* New York: Holiday House.

Web sites

http://www.bfree.on.ca/bow/prefix.html
Black on White

http://www.geocities.com/~les_novelist/webdoc2.htm
How to and Other Tips: Writing Novels, Books, Stories, Poetry

Editorial

Books

Kronenwetter, M. (1996). *How to write a news article.* Danbury, CT: Franklin Watts.

Lorenz, A. L. (1995). *News: Reporting and writing.* Needham Heights, MA: Allyn & Bacon.

Mencher, M. (1997). *News reporting and writing.* New York: McGraw Hill.

Web sites

http://www.ce.org/
Children's Express: By Children for Everybody

http://www.editorials.net
Editorials.Net

Essay

Books

Kirschenbuam, C. (1998). *How to write and sell your personal essays.* London, England: Davenport Productions.

McCall, J. (1998). *How to write themes and essays.* New York: Macmillan General Reference.

Web sites

http://www.cc.columbia.edu/acis/bartleby/strunk/
Elements of Style

http://www.teleport.com/~bjscript/index.htm
Essays on the Craft of Dramatic Writing

http://www.macarthur.uws.edu.au/ssd/ldc/essaywriting.html
How to Write an Essay

http://home1.gte.net/hmay/essay.htm
Tips on How to Write an Essay

http://www.sjsu.edu/faculty/patten/essay.htm
How to Write an Essay

Magazine

Books

Garcia, J. (1995). *Hispanic magazine: A publishing success story.* New York: Walker & Co.

Heller, S. (1996). *Magazines: Inside & out.* New York: PBC International.

Madama, J. (1993). *Desktop publishing: The art of communication.* Minneapolis, MN: Lerner Publishing Company.

Nelson, R. P. (1991). *Publication design.* Boston, MA: McGraw-Hill.

Web sites

http://www.geocities.com/Athens/Parthenon/3405
Magazine Writer's Network

http://www.theslot.com
The Slot: A Spot for Copy Editors

Newspaper

Books

Bentley, N. (1998). *The young journalist's book: How to write and produce your own newspaper.* Brookfield, CT: Millbrook Press.

Gibbons, G. (1987). *Deadline!: From news to newspaper.* New York: Ty Crowell.

Leedy, L. (1993). *The furry news: How to make a newspaper.* New York: Holiday House.

Lenhart, M. (1986). *Newspaper capers: Activities to acquaint students with newspapers.* Santa Barbara, CA: Learning Works.

Software

Classroom Newspaper Workshop CD-ROM
Tom Snyder Productions
80 Coolidge Hill Road
Watertown, MA 02472
Phone: (800) 342-0236

Web site

http://www.crockerfarm.org/ac/rm02/gazette/index.htm
Mrs. Streeter's Class Visits The Daily Hampshire Gazette Newspaper

Poem

Books

Drury, J. (1991). *Creating poetry.* Cincinnati, OH: Writers Digest Books.

Ferra, L. (1994). *A crow doesn't need a shadow: A guide to writing poetry from nature.* Layton, UT: Gibbs Smith Publisher.

Jerome, J. (1986). *The poet's handbook.* Cincinnati, OH: Writers Digest Books.

Kgositsile, K. (1994). *Approaches to poetry writing.* Chicago: Third World Press.

Kowit, S. (1995). *In the palm of your hand: A poet's portable workshop. A lively and illuminating guide for the practicing poet.* Gardiner, ME: Tilbury House Publishers.

Livingston, M. C. (1991). *Poem-making: Ways to begin writing poetry.* New York: Harpercollins Juvenile Books.

Oliver, M. (1995). *A poetry handbook.* Orlando, FL: Harcourt Brace.

Packard, W. (1992). *The art of poetry writing.* New York: St. Martins Printing.

Web sites

http://www.eml.jmu.edu/LAPS/LanguageArts/poetry/default.html
Study, Read, and Write Poetry

http://auden.websteruniv.edu/~osborsar/poetry.html
Da Poetry Page

http://www.writerswrite.com/poetry
Poetry Literature Resources and Resources for Poets

http://www.hypersven.com/poets.corner
Poet's Corner

Scientific Report

Books

Alley, M. (1996). *The craft of scientific writing.* New York: Springer Verlag.

Booth, V. (1993). *Communicating in science: Writing a scientific paper and speaking at scientific meetings.* New York: Cambridge University Press.

Day, R. A. (1998). *How to write and publish a scientific paper.* Phoenix, AZ: Oryx Press.

Gravois, M. (1998). *35 Ready-to-go ways to publish students' research and writing.* New York: Scholastic Professional Books Division.

Gubanich, A. A. (1997). *A student's guide to writing a scientific paper: How to survive the laboratory research report.* Dubuque, IA: Kendall/Hunt Publishing.

Sternberg, R. J. (1993). *The psychologist's companion: A guide to scientific writing for students and researchers.* New York: Cambridge University Press.

Web sites

http://www.sci-ed-ga.org/modules/k6/paper
The Scientific Research Paper

http://www.an.psu.edu/jxm57/sciwrit.html
Scientific Writing

Script

Books

Bentley, N. (1996). *Putting on a play: The young playwright's guide to scripting, directing, and performing.* Brookfield, CT: Millbrook Press.

British Library. (1998). *The British library guide to writing and scripts: History and techniques.* Toronto, ON: University of Toronto Press.

Cole, H. R. (1989). *The complete guide to standard script formats: The screenplay.* North Hollywood, CA: CMC Publishing.

Davis, R. (1998). *Writing dialogue for scripts.* Edinburgh: A & C Black.

Hatcher, J. (1996). *The art and craft of playwriting.* Cincinnati, OH: Story Press.

Phillips, W. H. (1991). *Writing short scripts.* Syracuse, NY: Syracuse University Press.

Seger, L. (1990). *Creating unforgettable characters.* New York: Henry Holt.

Seger, L. (1994). *Making a good script great.* New York: Samuel French Trade.

Straczynski, J. M. (1996). *The complete book of scriptwriting.* Cincinnati, OH: Writers Digest Books.

Willis, E. E. (1992). *Writing scripts for television, radio, and film.* San Diego, CA: HBJ College & School Division.

Software

Scriptware
Cinovation, Inc.
1750 30th St., Ste. 360
Boulder, CO 80301-1005
Phone: (800) 788-7090
Internet: http://scriptwritingsecrets.com

Web sites

http://www.asascreenwriters.com
American Screenwriters Association

http://elaine.teleport.com/~cdeemer/scrwriter.html
Screenwriters/Playwrights Homepage

http://www.writerswrite.com/screenwriting
Screenwriting—"Writers Write"

http://www.teleport.com/~cdeemer/scrwriter.html
Screenwriters and Playwrights Information

Books

Bauer, M. D. (1996). *Our stories: A fiction workshop from young authors.* New York: Clarion Books.

Bickham, J. M. (1994). *Writing the short story: A hands-on program.* Cincinnati, OH: Writers Digest Books.

Knight, D. (1997). *Creating short fiction.* New York: St. Martin's Press.

Kulpa, K., & Stahl, R. J. (1995). *Getting there: Seventh grade writing on life, school, and the universe.* East Greenwich, RI: Merlyn's Pen.

Sorenson, S. (1998). *How to write short stories* (3rd ed.). New York: Macmillan General Reference.

Software

The Amazing Writing Machine
Broderbund
P.O. Box 6121
Novato, CA 94948-6121
Phone: (415) 382-4700
Internet: http://www.broderbund.com

Storybuilder
Seven Valleys Software
Glen Rock, PA 17327
Phone: (800) 380-2717

StoryCraft
Fiction Writer's Software
StoryCraft Corporation.
909 Palm Ave., Ste. 109
Los Angeles, CA 90069
Phone: (800) 977-8679

Web sites

http://www.2learn.ca/currlinks/2teach/NetSplore/SWorkshop.html
Short Story Writing Workshop

http://www.inkspot.com
Inkspot: Writing Resources

Books

Davis, S. (1985). *The craft of lyric writing.* Cincinnati, OH: Writers Digest Books.

Fiarotta, N. (1993). *Music crafts for kids: The how-to book of music discovery.* Northampton, MA: Sterling Publications.

Mitchell, K. M. (1996). *Essential songwriters rhyming dictionary: Most practical and easy to use reference now available.* Van Nuys, CA: Alfred Publishing.

Wilson, C. (Ed.). (1996). *The Kingfisher young people's book of music.* New York: Kingfisher Books.

Zollo, P. (1997). *Songwriters on songwriting: The expanded version.* New York: Da Capo Printing.

Software

Music Chase1: The Music in Me
Tune 1000 Corp.
295 Forest Ave, Ste. 1000A
Portland, ME 04101-2000
Phone: (800) 363-8863

Web sites

http://www.writerswrite.com/songwriting
Songwriting—Songwriters Resource at Writers Write

http://www.english.uiuc.edu/cws/wworkshop/index.htm
UIUC Writer's Workshop

CHAPTER VIII

Multi-Categorical Products

For those products that combine two or more of the previously discussed categories, a separate designation has been established. Multi-categorical products include but are not limited to:

Broadcast	Multimedia Presentation
Campaign	Museum
Computer Program	News Cast
Documentary	Oral History
Exhibit	Television Show
Film	Time Capsule
Game	Video Game
Invention	Web Page

Following is an in-depth profile of eight selected multi-categorical products. Information presented includes: definitions, title of experts, types, words to know, helpful hints, exemplary producers, community resources, and quotes to inspire for each profiled product. This provided information should serve as a foundation. Students are strongly encouraged to add to the provided information as new knowledge and ideas are gained through the research and product development process. Grids that detail the components, characteristics, and basic materials for each of these products are also presented. In addition, authentic multi-categorical products created by students are highlighted. This chapter concludes with an informative bibliography of books, web sites, and software useful in developing multi-categorical products.

Product: Exhibit

Definition: A public show or display presented for others to view for the purpose of conveying information.

Title of the Expert: Exhibitor

Types of Exhibits:

Collectors	Interest Area
Commercial	Scientific
Historical	Sports

Words to Know:

Accordion	Paints
Back Lighting	Pantographs
Brush Finishing	Particle Board
Brushes	Permanent Bonding
Budget	Photographs
Cardboard	Photo Mats
Construction Paper	Plywood
Corkboard	Poster Paper
Corrugated Board	Project
Cutting Blades	Protractor
Decoration	Roller Painting
Easels	Signs
Ellipse Guides	Silk Screen
Flameproofing	Spackling
Floodlight	Spotlight
Foam-Core	Stencils
French Curve	Structure
Hardboard	T-Square
Headings	Tackboard
Hinges	Templates
Homosote	Theme
Indirect Lighting	Three-Dimensional
Ink	Tracing Paper
Island Arrangement	Triangle
Laquer Spray	Triptych
Lettering	Two-Dimensional
Motion Displays	Typography
Mounting Fabrics	Upson Board
Mounting Rubber Cement	Valance

Open-Book Arrangement   Warpage
Overlay Sheets

Helpful Hints:

- Make a decision about the structural form for the exhibit.
- Be sure to title the exhibit.
- Produce a written summary of the exhibit.
- Brief statements on cards should be placed at key areas of the exhibit.
- Work on a plan of things to be accomplished and a realistic time table.
- Photographs look better and attract more attention when framed by a mat.
- Narration, if present, should be clear and concise.

Exemplary Producers:

Louis Danziger	Paul Rudolph
Aris Kanstantinides	Lisbeth Sachs
Paul McCobb	Tapio Wirkkala
Nelly Rudin	

Community Resources:
Visual Merchandising Specialist, Graphic Designers, Museum Curator, Art Gallery Director, Trade Show Designer, Science Fair Coordinator

Quotes to Inspire:

"Give me a museum and I'll fill it."

—Pablo Picasso

"That which, perhaps, hears more nonsense
than anything in the world,
is a picture in a muse.

—Goncourt Edmond de and Jules

Product Criteria Grid

Product: Exhibit

Components	*Characteristics*	*Basic Materials*
Theme or Title	• Self-explanatory, clearly states purpose of exhibit	Audio Tape Backdrop Construction Paper Display Cases Index Cards Markers Paint Poster Board Table Coverings Tables Tape Recorder
Location	• Neat, legible, concise, correct spelling and grammar, corresponds with display items	
Graphics/Photos	• Clear, attractive, appropriate to theme and audience	
Materials/Display Items	• Topic-related, interactive (optional), durable, interesting, high quality, authentic (if possible)	
Narration	• Knowledge of topic evident, audible, pleasant voice, emphasis placed on important points	

Product: Game

Definition: An activity, often competitive, in which players contend with each other according to a set of rules.

Title of Expert: Designer/Inventor

Types of Games:

Board	Positional
Card	Race
Dexterity	Simulation
Dice	Strategy
Domino	String
Folder	Video
Mancala	War
Number	Word

Words to Know:

Adjacent	Marker
Alternate	Mill
Backward	Move
Clockwise	Object
Complexity	Opponent
Counters	Penalty
Crown	Player
Dealer	Points
Diagonal Move	Rules
Die	Score
Doubled	Spaces
Draw	Spinner
Equipment	Strategy
Flank	Tactic
Forward	Tally
Homebase	Team
Huff	Teetotum
Maneuver	Tie
Manipulation	Turn

Helpful Hints:

- Match the game to the interests and abilities of the intended user.
- Make rules clear and simple.

- A game should offer a variety of possibilities to prevent boredom.
- Design games that stimulate the imagination and also teach.
- Be sure to have a suggested number of players.
- Pennies, buttons, and seeds make excellent playing pieces.
- Have a method for determining who will move first (i.e., flipping a coin or rolling a die).
- Medium-weight cardboard from gift boxes makes excellent board game bases.
- Game boards can be made of paper, cardboard, wood, stone, and so forth.

Exemplary Producers:

Jeffrey Breslow	Howard Morrison
James Brunot	Edward P. Parker
Alfred M. Butts	George S. Parker
Charles B. Darrow	James J. Shea, Sr.
Thomas J. Kalinske	Rouben Terzian
Lizzie J. Magie	

Community Resources: Graphic Designer, Toy Store Owner, Peers

Quote to Inspire:

"I recently learned something quite interesting about video games. Many young people have developed incredible hand, eye, and brain coordination in playing these games. The air force believes these kids will be our outstanding pilots should they fly our jets."

—Ronald Reagan

Product Criteria Grid

Product: Game

Components	Characteristics	Basic Materials
Title	• Legible, neat, correct spelling and grammar, original, related to concept	Cardboard Computer Index Cards Markers Paper Poster Board Scissors
Concept	• Original, related to topic/theme	
Directions	• Legible, clearly stated, purpose of game defined, systematic, thorough	
Complexity	• Appropriate for intended audience/players, requires strategy	
Rules	• Legible, clearly stated, easy to understand, reasonable	
Playing Pieces	• Easy to differentiate, durable, appropriate to game	
Design/Layout	• Aesthetically appealing, neat, uncluttered, durable	

Product: Invention

Definition: An original product designed to solve a problem in a creative manner.

Title of Expert: Inventor

Types of Inventions:

Conservation	Innovative
Convenience	Safety
Fun	Useful
Health	Work-Saving

Words to Know:

Brainstorming	Marketing
Copyright	Model
Creative Problem Solving	Originality
Design	Patent
Directions	Patent Lawyer
Disclosure Forms	Piggybacking
Divergent Thinking	Planning
Elaboration	Problem
Fact	Prototype
Flexibility	Record Keeping
Fluency	Sketch
Idea	Solution
Imagination	Trademark

Helpful Hints:

- Keep it simple and modify an existing invention.
- Invent something needed by you, your friends, and family.
- Keep detailed records in an invention notebook.
- Give the invention an interesting name.
- Make the invention durable and attractive.
- Establish a place to work.

Exemplary Producers:

John Bardeen	Grace Hopper
Jocelyn Burnbell	Robert Jarvick
Chester Carlson	Alec Jeffreys
Thomas Edison	John H. Kellogg

Gertrude Elion
George W. Ferris, Jr.
D. Henry Ford
Benjamin Franklin
Galileo Galilei
Chester Greenwood
Ruth Handler
Elizabeth Hazen

Margaret Knight
Edward Land
Fred Morrison
Jonas Salk
Susan Solomon
Jan B. Svochak
Levi Strauss

Community Resources: Inventors, Scientists, Marketing Specialist, Patent Attorney, Patent Holder

Quotes to Inspire:

"Inventing is a combination of brains and materials.
The more brains you use, the less materials you need."
—Charles F. Kettering

"Invention breeds invention."
—Ralph Waldo Emerson

"To be an inventor you must let your mind search,
to think of many possible solutions to each invention problem you encounter."
—Steven Coney

"Imagination is more important than knowledge."
—Albert Einstein

"An invention does not have be a new machine or something that will change the world.
An invention may be an old idea with a new twist or improvement."
—Lauren DeLuca

"To invent, you need a good imagination and a pile of junk."
—Thomas Edison

Save a Child Box

by Patrick Knape

Patrick Knape, a 14-year-old student at Danbury Middle School, lives in the small Gulf coastal town of Danbury, TX. He assists with the family crop dusting service, raises and shows animals, plays basketball, likes TV, drawing, and rodeo team roping. His educational plans will prepare him for becoming a zoologist.

The Save a Child box was designed as a device to save children's lives, to keep adults from being shot, and to prevent gun theft. In my research, it was discovered that guns often were not hidden properly, and are easily accessed by children or found by potential thieves. Because of this, my purpose was to invent a product to conceal guns and, at the same time, warn responsible parties of tampering with the gun storage unit. After looking at sporting goods stores that sell guns, I found that the only safety devices were trigger locks requiring a key that could be lost. My first thought was that a box with a sound warning would deter a child or thief and warn reliable adults. My belief was that some sort of beeping sound would be enough to scare children and they would stop before handling the gun. After discussing the idea with my dad, it was decided that a louder warning signal could alert adults as well as scare a child.

We surveyed several different sounding devices at the local Radio Shack and decided on one where a button, when released, triggers the alarm. First, I got a box at a neighborhood grocery store free of charge that I painted prior to beginning the wiring process. The ends of the wires had to be soldered to the switch, and the alarm and the different wires from the alarm switch to the battery connector. Then, the connections between the alarm and the battery and the button switch had to be fitted and taped. Next, the switch was mounted at the opening end of the box so that, upon lifting the lid, the alarm would be triggered. The switch button was placed in a cardboard shelf cut to fit the box. To serve as a padding in the bottom of the box, a piece of thick foam was used. After all parts were assembled and a toy gun (designated with an orange tip) was put into place, the battery was connected and tucked under the shelf. It was necessary to check the box periodically for battery life. Finally, a little knob was attached for a handle on the outside of the box labeled with "Save a Child" using stick-on letters.

My general concern for the numerous deaths caused by guns not being hidden safely from children prompted my idea and development of this product. Personal safety and science were incorporated in developing the Save a Child Box.

My product was entered in the 1996–97 Brazoria County Science Fair. It won first place in Overall Inventions, Best of Show over the entire age groups, and a First Place Gold medal for the entire event held in Angleton, TX. Results of the fair were published in the *Angleton Times* and the *Brazospart Facts*.

My product worked as I'd planned and may inspire other young inventors. It is my hope that it will save more lives. I learned a little more about soldering and wiring for sound, discovering the sound part was pretty difficult to get to work.

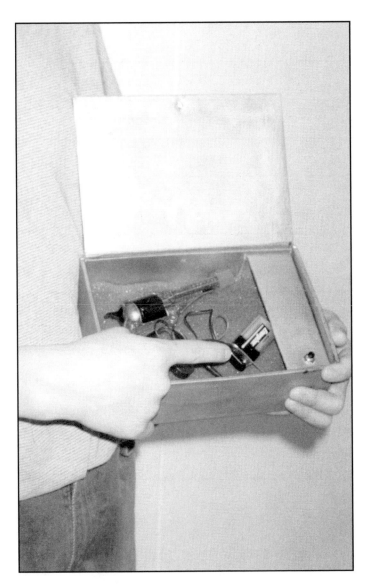

Patrick demonstrates the operation of The Save A Child box.

Product Criteria Grid

Product: Invention

Components	*Characteristics*	*Basic Materials*
Idea	• Original, creative	Computer File Folder Legal Documents Markers Paper Pencil Rulers Various Materials
Purpose	• Clearly stated, useful, creatively solves a problem	
Sketch	• Accurate, to scale, detailed, neat	
Prototype (model)	• Representative, well-constructed	
Materials	• Durable, appropriate to invention	
Name/Title	• Interesting, appealing to intended audience, easy to remember	
Patent/Trademark	• Well-researched, appropriate documentation	
Marketing	• Clearly communicated to potential consumer, original, attention-getting	

Product: Multimedia Slide Show

Definition: The process of combining computer-generated graphic images with video and sound to create an interactive presentation.

Title of Expert: Multimedia Specialist

Types of Multimedia Slide Shows:

Continuous-Run	Scripted
Interactive	

Words to Know:

Animation	LCD Projector
Audio	Mouse
Box-In	Narration
Box-Out	Navigate
Build	Notes
Bullet	Organization
Button	Overhead
CD-ROM	Platform
Charts	Point-and-Click
Cursor	Point Size
Cut	Powerpoint
Digital Camera	Quicktime
Dissolve	Run-Time
Effects	Scanner
Fade	Screen
Flow	Scroll
Font	Slide
Graphics	Storyboard
Home	Template
Hot Spot	Text
HyperCard	Title
Hyperlink	Transition
Icon	Tutorial
Keyboard	Video
Layout	Wipes
LCD Panel	

Helpful Hints:

- Before you begin, know exactly what you want to communicate.

- Make sure every slide adds to the presentation. Eliminate unnecessary slides.
- Use a template to keep style and background consistent.
- Keep slides simple. Avoid clutter and keep effects to a minimum.
- Use no smaller than 24-point type.
- Know your presentation software's capabilities and limitations.
- Compose your presentation as a diagram map prior to entering it on the computer.
- Consider the audience before you prepare the presentation. Tailor your presentation to meet their needs.
- Check location of electrical outlets in the room where you will be presenting. Always bring an extension cord and tape to secure the cord for safety.
- Set up and test all equipment on-site before delivering your presentation.
- Handouts can be a valuable addition to your presentation.
- Be prepared to shift presentation flow and direction in response to audience.
- Remember, older LCD panels require the room to be substantially darkened for viewing.
- Take classes on the software you will be using. This will save time, and you will make better-looking presentations.
- Use phrases and key words, not sentences.
- Remember to turn off the screensaver before beginning.
- Have a back-up plan ... make overheads of your presentation.

Exemplary Producers:

Tim Fleck	Roger Wagner
Doug Lowe	Emily Sherrill Weadock
Margaret Rabb	Glenn E. Weadock
Brian Reilly	

Community Resources: Media Specialist, Computer Teacher, Local Advertising Agency, Television Stations, Newspapers

Quotes to Inspire:

"The person who uses yesterday's tools in today's work won't be in business tomorrow."

—Anonymous

"The most brilliant colors, spread at random and without design, will give far less pleasure than the simplest outline of a figure."

—Aristotle

"Things seen are mightier than things heard."

—Alfred Lord Tennyson

Product Criteria Grid

Product: Multimedia Slide Show

Components	Characteristics	Basic Materials
Title	• Corresponds with topic, captures audience attention	Computer LCD Panels Microphones Paper Pencil Presentation Software Projector Resource Books Screen Speakers
Content	• Suitable for intended audience, informative, accurate, relevant	
Organization	• Logical, allows for audience interaction	
Transitions	• Smooth, visually appealing, appropriate for mood and audience	
Graphics	• Clear, corresponds with content, appropriate to audience/mood	
Sound/Animation (optional)	• Not distracting, enhances content, appropriately timed to correspond with text	
Design	• Principles of design employed (i.e., balance, contrast, variety, etc.) not cluttered, neat, easy to read	
Color	• Attractive, easy on the eye, contrasts for ease in reading, appropriate for topic/audience	

Product: Oral History

Definition: A method of gathering and preserving historical information through recorded interviews with participants from past events and ways of life.

Title of Expert: Historian

Types of Oral History:

Audio
Autobiographical
Biographical
Community
Elite
Event

Family
Historical
Non-Elite
Photographic
Video

Words to Know:

Accounts
Accuracy
Ancestor
Archive
Artifacts
Autobiography
Biography
Census
Certificates
Clippings
Data
Diary
Document
Epitaph
Event
Evidence

Experiences
Geneaology
Interview
Issues
Lineage
Memory
Notes
Obituary
Records
Reliable Source
Surname
Time Line
Transcription
Wills
Witness

Helpful Hints:

- Before interviewing, have a clearly defined topic or theme.
- Prepare a biographical file on the subjects to be interviewed.
- Use a tape recorder or video camcorder during interviews.
- Ask questions that require more than a "yes" or "no" response.
- Use abbreviations when note taking, but fill in the blanks as soon after the interview as possible while your memory is still fresh.
- If you are recording your family history, interview your oldest living relative first.

- Prior to the interview, ask the person to begin gathering old photos and documents that will help them remember the time period you wish to discuss.
- Put your questions on numbered index cards.
- Arrive on time and select an area free of noise and other distractions in which to conduct the interview.
- Make the person you are interviewing comfortable.
- Check the accuracy of all data obtained from sources.
- When transcribing the interview, include both the questions asked and the responses to the questions.
- Important information can often be obtained from photographs. Use a magnifying glass to get a more detailed analysis.
- Handle all documents and photographs with care.
- Tax records, land records, wills, birth and death certificates, family Bibles, diaries, old letters, newspapers, old telephone directories, and cemeteries are all sources of information.
- Place copies of your interview in a library or archive. Never underestimate the historical significance of what you have recorded. As time passes, it will become more valuable and unique.

Exemplary Producers:

James Truslow Adams	Samuel Eliot Morison
Hubert H. Bancroft	Allan Nevins
Henry Thomas Buckle	Francis Parkman
Edward Channing	James Ford Rhodes
Ssuma Ch'ien	Studs Terkel
Herodotus	Barbara Wertheim Tuchman
Margaret Kernochan Leech	Thucydides

Community Resources: Archivist, Historian, Historical Society, Librarian, Family Members, Adults, Friends

Quotes to Inspire:

"Anybody can make history.
Only a great man can write it."

—Oscar Wilde

"To a historian libraries are food, shelter, and even muse.
They are of two kinds: the library of published material, books, pamphlets, periodicals, and the archive of unpublished papers and documents."

—Barbara Tuchman

"History is a record of human progress, a record of the struggle of the advancement of the human mind, of the human spirit, toward some known or unknown objective."

—Jawaharlal Nehru

"History is the version of past events that people have decided to agree upon."

—Napoleon Bonaparte

Shimmeree Magazine

by Matt Vine, Joshua Newcombe, Nathanual Scott, Richard Austin, & Bryan House

Matt Vine is a freshman at Newark High School in Newark, NY. He is working with a small group of students to produce the third issue of Shimmeree Magazine *which highlights stories based on authentic historical accounts from the local area.*

This story began three years ago when we were in seventh grade. The enrichment program at the middle school invited interested students to participate in a project that would produce some kind of publication based on oral history research. That project was completed with the production of the first issue of *Shimmeree: A Community Reflection on Life and Work Along the Erie Canal.* Jadwiga Biskupska, Andrew Boeckmann, Holly Conklin, Anthony Hess, Bryan House, Joshua Newcombe, Michael Schaefer, Nathanual Scott, and myself carried the project into a second year and produced *Shimmeree: Book II: A Community Reflection on Ghosts, the Holocaust, and Future Images of the Environment.* Furthermore, some of us are still continuing the project and are working toward *Shimmeree: Book III.*

We put our product in the form of a magazine because we believe this format will expose the information to many people and will become part of the written historical record of the area. These are real stories that will be lost when people are gone, and they need to be preserved. Since publication, *Shimmeree* has been included in our local historical archives and library collections. Consideration is being given to creating a web site to the put the information on the Internet so it is available to more people. However, the magazine format allows persons of all ages, with and without computers, access to what has been written.

The project involved a first-hand investigation into local history. The articles were based on oral history interviews in areas of our choice: ghosts, the Holocaust, and future images of the environment. The subject areas incorporated were English/language arts, social studies, arts, and technology. Skills related to self-direction, creativity, research, and group work were also developed. As we progressed through the project, needed skills were learned to produce the final product. For example, we became more self-directed: brainstorming and choosing ideas, developing plans for implementation of the project, and setting time lines for the work.

Each of the magazines contains original creative writing related to themes. Professional writers provided some creative inspiration and direction. They taught us to choose words carefully, to create better sentence structure, and to use words to develop images in the readers' minds. We also learned how to prepare ourselves and organize the materials that would be used in the interviews with the contact people. Working in groups helped us learn that, in order for the work to get done, responsibilities had to be shared, and persistence was necessary to meet deadlines. The mood of our work was enhanced through the use of photographs. Certain moods related to the written pieces were brainstormed, and then photographs were taken to enhance the writing.

Although we continuously self-evaluate the magazine to determine what is good and what needs work, the best evaluation comes from our readers. They have given us very positive responses, especially those individuals highlighted within the magazine. We gained a lot of satisfaction knowing that true-life stories have been preserved that pertain to events in our area, and these people have also gained from sharing such stories with us.

Advice to others would be prepare for hard work and be committed to what you are attempting to do. In addition, create guidelines and a schedule for work. If you are going to work in teams, make sure that everyone is as devoted or more devoted than you are. The quote to be shared is by Benjamin Disraeli who stated: "Man is made to create, from the poet to the potter."

SHIMMEREE ASSOCIATES 1997–1998: (counter clockwise) Richard Austin, Matthew Vine, Joshua Newcombe, and Bryan House. Not pictured is Nathanual Scott.

Product Criteria Grid

Product: Oral History

Components	Characteristics	Basic Materials
Title	• Appropriate to theme/content, comprehensive, yet concise	Camcorder Camera Computer Data Sheets Index Cards Magnifying Glass Notebook Paper Pencil Public Records Tape Recorder
Investigation	• Thorough, use of multiple sources of information (print and nonprint), well-planned, formulation of broad-based questions	
Documentation	• Thorough, appropriate citation of sources, neat, legible, accurate, correct spelling and grammar	
Sources	• Reliable, use of both primary and secondary, authentic, related to topic/content, credible, substantiated	
Photographs (optional)	• Clear, enhancing, authentic	
Artifacts	• Relevant to topic, enhancing, interesting	

Product: Television Show

Definition: A program combining pictures and sound for view in various formats on a specific topic.

Title of Expert: Producer, Director

Types of Television Shows:

Animated/Cartoons	Interview
Awards Show	Music Program
Documentary	News Broadcast
Drama	Political Debates
Editorial	Serial
Educational	Sitcom
Financial Report	Sportscast
Game Shows	Talk Show
Instructional	Variety Show

Words to Know:

Actors	Host
Adapter	Instant Replay
Air	Lavalieres
Anchor	Lens
Announcer	Lighting
Audio	Microphone
Audio Technician	Middle Ground
Background	Miniatures
Broadcaster	Mixers
Cable	Monitor
Camcorder	Network
Camera	Pan
Camera Operator	Producer
Censorship	Rating
Character	Record
Close-Up	Satellite
Commercial	Script
Control Room	Segment
Copyright	Set
Credits	Sound
Cut	Split Screen
Director	Sponsors
Dissolve	Storyboard
Dolly	Studio

Editing	Switcher/Mixer
Film	Tape
Footage	Teleprompter
Foreground	Title
Generators	Tripod
Graphics	Video
Headphones	Viewers

Helpful Hints:

- Fast forward and rewind videocassettes before initial use.
- Store the master and circulate the duplicate.
- Use the slipcovers provided with the videocassette, as dust can damage the VCR.
- Always use headphones to monitor the audio.
- Arrange and test your equipment before use.
- Beware of using too many pans and zooms.
- Become aware of copyright laws.
- Determine the cost of your production prior to beginning.
- Write your script to the interest and level of your audience.
- Graphics should support and reinforce your audio/video.

Exemplary Producers:

Lucille Ball	Jerry Seinfeld
Bill Cosby	Rod Serling
Robert Flaherty	Aaron Spelling
Merv Griffin	Ted Turner
Edward Murrow	Oprah Winfrey
Carl Sagan	

Community Resources: Local TV Station, Anchor Persons, Cable Company, Media Specialist, Radio/TV/Communications Department at College or University, Consumer

Quotes to Inspire:

"In television we have the greatest instrument for mass persuasion in the history of the world."
—Budd Schulberg

"Television is becoming a collage—there are so many channels that you move through them making a collage yourself. In that sense, everyone sees something a bit different."
—David Hockney

"If it weren't for electricity we'd all be watching television by candlelight."
—George Gobel

Product Criteria Grid

Product: Television Show

Components	Characteristics	Basic Materials
Title	• Reflects content, appealing to intended audience, concise, original	Camcorder Computer Cue Cards Microphones Paper Pencil Script Set Design/Backdrop
Content	• Significant to intended audience, accurate, engaging, thought-provoking	
Dialogue	• Audible, enhancing, appropriate vocabulary for intended audience, appropriate dialects (if applicable)	
Action	• Enhancing, appropriate to content	
Props/Scenery/ Costumes	• Realistic, historically correct, not distracting	
Credits	• All-inclusive, prominently displayed, timed for readability, accurate recognition of responsibilities	
Commercials (optional)	• In good taste, nonoffensive, appropriate to audience, informative, appealing	

Product: Video

Definition: A cinematic narrative prepared for viewing by telecast, videocassette, video disc, and so forth.

Title of Expert: Videographer, Cinematographer

Types of Videos:

Aerial	Music
Animated	Narrative
Autobiographical	Satirical
Computerized	Surrealistic
Documentary	Undersater
Fantasy	

Words to Know:

AC Adapter	Gaffer
Amplifier	Grip
Angle	Location
Audio Mixer	Log
Backdrop	Long Play (LP)
Battery Recharger	Make-Up
Black and White	Microphone
Boom	Pan
Budget	Pixilation
Camcorder	Props
Camera	RCA Cables
Close-up	Rehearsal
Color	Rewind
Copyright	RF Splitter
Costumes	Scene
Credits	Screen
Cue	Screening
Dialogue	Script
Dub	Set
Edit	Shoot
Exposure	Slow Motion
Extended Play (EP)	Sound
Extreme Shots	Special Effects
Fade-In	Splice
Fade-Out	Standard Play (SP)
Fast Forward	Storyboard

Film Lenses	Subtitles
Focus	Synchronize
Footage	Tripod
Format	TV Monitor
Frame	VCR
Freeze Frame	VHS

Helpful Hints:

- Read the instruction booklet for your videocamera carefully and refer to it often.
- Expose at least five seconds of video for each title so your audience has enough time to read it.
- Make sure the scenery and costumes are historically accurate. For example, there should be no telephone wires in videos representing medieval times.
- Before you begin filming, plan your procedure on a storyboard.
- Be sure to synchronize sound with visuals.
- Don't be angle crazy!
- Rehearse, rehearse, rehearse.

Exemplary Producers:

Ingmar Bergman	Fritz Lang
Wendy Clarke	Friedrich Wilhelm Murnau
Caleb Deschanel	Nam June Paik
Karl Freud	Charles Rosher
Lee Garmes	Steven Spielberg
Jean-Luc Godard	Joseph Von Sternberg
David Wark Griffith	Francois Truffant
Alfred Hitchcock	Orson Welles
James Wong Howe	Lina Wertmüller
Akira Kurosawa	

Community Resources: Camera Store, TV Camera Man, Media Specialist, Professional Photographers

Quotes to Inspire:

"Film music should have the same relationship to the film drama
that somebody's piano playing in my living room has to the book I am reading.
—Igor Stravinsky

"A film is a petrified fountain of thought."

—Jean Cocteau

Product Criteria Grid

Product: Video

Components	Characteristics	Basic Materials
Title	• Representative of theme/topic, easy to remember, interesting	Actor/Actress Camcorder Computer Microphone Paper Pencil Scenery Script Tripod Videotape
Visuals	• Clear, representative of the topic, capture viewer's interest	
Audio	• Clear, audible, coordinated with visuals	
Editing	• Enhances visuals and audio, smooth transitions	
Special Effects/Graphics	• Skillfully executed, enhances video, consideration of design elements (i.e., balance, emphasis, variety, contrast, etc.)	
Credits	• Appropriate acknowledgments, legible, suitably timed for viewer reading	

Product: Web Site

Definition: A set of conceptually related, interlinked pages designed for use on the Internet.

Title of Expert: Webmaster, Site Engineer, Site Designer

Types of Web Sites:

Business	Marketing
Entertainment	Organization
Informative	Personal
Interest Area	

Words to Know:

Animation	JPEG
Archive	Layout
Avatar	Link
AVI	Macromedia
Background	MBONE
Bitmap	Memory
Body	MIDI
Bookmarks	MIME
Browser	Modem
Button	MPEG
Cache	Navigation
CD-ROM	OLE
CGI	Online
Clip Art	Pagemaker
Color	Panel
Compression	PDF
Concept	Ping
Configurations	Plug-in
Connection	PNG Interactive
Cursor	Port
Directory	Programming
Download	Quicktime
E-mail	Screen
File	Scripting Language
Font	Search Engine
Frame	Server
FTP	Shockwave
GIF	Site
Gopher	Storyboard

Graphics	Surfing
Head	Tags
Hit	TCP/IP
Host	Telnet
HTML	Upload
HTTP	URL
Hyperlinks	VRML
Image	WAIS
Interface	Webmaster
Internet Protocol	Window
Java	WWW
JavaScript	

Helpful Hints:

- Determine who your potential audience will be so that you can make your design relevant and aesthetically appealing to them.
- Determine the content your web site will display prior to production.
- Map out the navigation organization for your site. Storyboarding or the construction of a branching diagram will assist in this process.
- Create a prototype, such as an on-screen slide show, first.
- Use software that works and has a good track record.
- Keep the latest editions of books relating to web design on hand for quick reference.
- Test your site on friends before uploading to a host server.
- Register your site with the appropriate online directories and search engines.
- Use the largest typeface that works (10-point, 12-point, or larger) and keep the number of different typefaces to a minimum.
- Communicate with clarity. Use common syntax.
- Avoid clutter.
- Use color to denote text that links to other areas.
- Remember, the web should be used to provide useful information.
- Make sure you update your site periodically to keep it fresh.
- Review web sites in a topic/subject area in which you are interested.

Exemplary Producers:

Arthur Bebak	Bill Gates
Tim Berners-Lee	David Siegel
Jack Davis	Bud E. Smith

Community Resources: Computer Teacher, Professor of Technology, Local Web Site Developers

Quotes to Inspire:

"The front page is your first chance. This is where people have to decide whether they want to use your site or not."

—Matthew Butterick

"A year ago, everything was flat and static. Now we have pages that are dynamically generated, based on the user's software and input."

—Jeff Venn

"Design for the web is a real art in itself."

—Jonathan Nelson

"Looking at the proliferation of personal web pages on the net, it looks like very soon everyone on Earth will have 15 Megabytes of fame."

—M.G. Siriam

"URL's are the 800 numbers of the 1990's"

—Chris Clark

Photography Web Site
by Ellery Loomis and Jason Laing

 *Ellery Loomis and Jason Laing are both 12 years old and in the seventh grade at George Fox Middle School in Pasadena, MD. Ellery likes photography, soccer, basketball, baseball, and lacrosse and is also a member of the Pasadena Boy Scout Troop #773. Jason has been a member of his school's Odyssey of the Mind team for the past two years.*

When we took our cameras to Downs Park as part of the enrichment program, we didn't know something so big would come from something so small. It all started when we were listening to Ms. Schupp, our school's enrichment teacher, on how to take good photos. She taught us some basics of photography in an introductory lesson. Afterward, we went off with our group to take pictures in the park. After the pictures were developed, we examined our successes and failures and wound up matting enlargements to enter into a contest. We both placed in the county media festival. However, we wanted to do something more. Jason wanted to learn how to make a web page, and I (Ellery) wanted to have a lot more fun by making a project on photography that would help other beginning photographers. The first step was to organize our thoughts by making a graphic organizer. We decided to include some dos and don'ts in our project, along with sample photos. Selecting pictures to use was a tiring task because we had over 50 from which to choose.

To develop the web page, computer graphics, Netscape Editor, and a PC were used in the enrichment room. Ms. Schupp taught us how to create a web page. We thought that this was one of the hardest parts of our project. People who visit this web site will learn about lens flare, bird's-eye-view, ant's-eye-view, human-eye-view, distracting objects, the creators of the web site, and Ms. Schupp.

As we worked on this project, we used skills in art, language arts for text, math to proportion pictures, and technology education with the computer. Our project was shown at the school's Showcase Night when families and incoming fifth graders attended to see what students at our school have accomplished. We also were videotaped by the gifted and talented office so other schools would learn about this project. Our largest audience is the World Wide Web. In evaluating we asked ourselves: Does this product appeal to a wide audience? Is it easy to use? Is it appealing? Does it represent accurate information?

As a result of our work, we acquired skills in photography, interviewing, HTML, organization, and communication. For others thinking about doing involved projects, I say you should expect it to take a long time and always expect something to go wrong! Jason thinks, the best way to inspire learning is with other forms of learning. Remember, learning doesn't always have to occur in the regular classroom, but it is a good place to start exploring your ideas. You can visit our web site at: http://www.aacps.org/aacps/gfms/Photo0.htm/.

Product Criteria Grid

Product: Web Site

Components	Characteristics	Basic Materials
Title	• Representative of topic/theme, prominent, appealing, concise	Books Computer Information Internet Paper Pencil Printer Web Construction Software Kits
Home Page	• Aesthetically appealing, attention-grabbing, accurate, informative	
Links	• Related to topic/theme, enhancing	
Graphics	• Clear, correspond with text, uncluttered, relevant	
Layout	• Logically organized, user-friendly, neat	
Content	• Relevant to intended audience, accurate, reliable, in good taste, comprehensive	

Multi-Categorical Resources

Exhibit

Books

Art Calendar. (Ed.) (1998). *Getting exposure: The artist's guide to exhibiting the work.* Rockville, MD: The Lyons Press.

Cooper, H., Hegarty, P., Hegarty, P., & Simco, N. (Eds.). (1996). *Display in the classroom: Principles, practice and learning theory.* London, England: David Fulton Publishing.

Jackson, M. (1994). *Creative display and environment.* Portsmouth, NJ: Heinemann.

Neal, A. (1987). *Help for the small museum: Handbook of exhibit ideas and methods.* Boulder, CO: Pruett Publishing.

Serrell, B. (1996). *Exhibit labels: An interpretive approach.* Keyport, NJ: Altamira Printing.

Skaggs, G. (1993). *Bulletin boards and displays: Good ideas for librarians and teachers.* Jefferson, NC: McFarland & Company.

Web site

http://www.si.edu
Smithsonian Institution

Game

Books

Dugan, R. (Ed.). (1993). *Best board games from around the world.* Columbus, OH: Highlights for Children.

Pearson, C. (1982). *Make your own games workshop.* Carthage, IL: Fearon Teacher Aids.

Provenzo, A. B., & Provenzo, E. F. (1981). *Favorite board games you can make and play.* New York: Dover Publications.

Web sites

http://www.crossover.com/~costik/nowords.html
I Have No Words and I Must Design

http://www.neversoft.com/christer/GR/design
Computer Game Design

Invention

Books

Bender, L. (1991). *Invention.* New York: Knopf.

Bloch, S. (1994). *Selling your idea or invention: The birthplace-to-marketplace guide.* Secaucus, NJ: Birch Lane Printing.

Erlbach, A. (1999). *The kids' invention book.* Minneapolis, MN: Lerner Publications Company.

Karnes, F. A., & Bean, S. M. (1995). *Girls and young women inventing: Twenty true stories about inventors plus how you can be one yourself.* Minneapolis, MN: Free Spirit Publishing.

Software

The Genius of Edison
The Learning Company
One Athenaeum St.
Cambridge, MA 02477
Phone: (800) 973-5111
Internet: http://www.learningco.com

InventorLabs
Houghton Mifflin Interactive
120 Beacon St.
Somerville, MA 02143
Phone: (617) 351-3333
Internet: http://www.hmco.com/hmi

Web sites

http://www.invent.org
Inventure Place

http://www.uspto.gov
Patent and Trademark Office

Multimedia Slide Show

Books

Brown, A. L. (1997). *Power pitches: How to produce winning presentations using charts, slides, video and multimedia.* Burr Ridge, IL: Irwin Professional Publishers.

Rabb, M. (1993). *The presentation design book: Tips, techniques and advice for creating effective, attractive slides, overheads, multimedia presentations, screen shows.* Research Triangle Park, NC: Ventana Communications Group.

Robbins, J. (1997). *High-impact presentations: A multimedia approach.* New York: John Wiley & Sons.

Software

HyperStudio/Roger Wagner Productions
1050 Pioneer Way, Ste. P
El Cajon, CA 92020
Phone: (800) 497-3778

Powerpoint Presentation Software
Microsoft Corporation
One Microsoft Way
Redmond, WA 98052-6399
Phone: (425) 882-8080
Internet: http://www.microsoft.com/powerpoint

Web sites

http://www.computertips.com/Microsoftoffice/MsPowerPoint/aheader.htm
Powerpoint Tips

http://www.javierlopez.com/new.html
Slide Show Multimedia Presentations

Oral History

Books

Ives, E. D. (1995). *The tape-recorded interview: A manual for fieldworkers in folklore and oral history.* Knoxville, TN: University of Tennessee Printing.

Ritchie, D. A. (1994). *Doing oral history.* Boston, MA: Twayne Publications.

Smith, L. (1996). *Oral history.* New York: Ballantine Books.

Spence, L. (1997). *Legacy: A step-by-step guide to writing personal history.* Columbus, OH: Ohio University Press.

Web sites

http://www.baylor.edu/~OHA/Welcome.html
Oral History Association

http://www.lineagesnet.com/active/query/index.htm
Lineages' Free Queries

http://www.oz.net/~cyndihow/sites.htm
Cyndi's List of Genealogy Sites on the Internet

http://www.genealogy.org/~uvpafug/fhlslc.html
Family History Centers

http://www.familytreemaker.com/index.html
Family Tree Maker's Genealogy Site

http://genealogy.emcee.com
Genealogy Online

http://www.global.org/bfreed/geneol/gen-soft.html
Genealogy Software

Television Show

Books

Harmon, R. (1994). *The beginning filmmaker's business guide: Financial, legal, marketing, and distribution basics of making movies.* New York: Walker & Co.

Limousin, O. (1993). *TV and films: Behind the scenes.* Ossining, NY: Young Discovery Library.

Miller, M. (1996). *Behind the scenes at the TV news studio.* Austin, TX: Raintree/Steck Vaughn.

O'Brien, L. (1998). *Lights, camera, action! Making movies and TV from the inside out.* Toronto: Owl Communications.

Web sites

http://www.emmys.org/tindex.html
Academy of Television Arts and Sciences

http://www.cpb.org
Corporation for Public Broadcasting

http://www.mtr.org
Museum of Television and Radio

Video

Books

Bentley, N. (1995). *The young producer's video book: How to write, direct, and shoot your own video.* Brookfield, CT: Millbrook Press.

Frantz, J. P. (1994). *Video cinema: Techniques and projects for beginning filmmakers.* Chicago: Chicago Review Press.

O'Brien, L. (1998). *Lights, camera, action! Making movies and TV from the inside out.* Toronto: Owl Communications.

Videomaker Magazine. (1996). *The videomaker handbook: A comprehensive guide to making video.* Boston, MA: Focal Press.

Software

Write, Camera, Action
Broderbund Software Inc.
500 Redwood Blvd.
P.O. Box 6125
Novato, CA 94948-6125
Phone: (415) 382-4700
Internet: http://www.broaderbund.com

Web site

http://www.videomaker.com
Videomaker's Camcorder and Desktop Video Site

Web Site

Books

Lampton, C. F. (1997). *Home page: An introduction to web page design.* Danbury, CT: Franklin Watts.

Lopuck, L. (1997). *Kid's web kit.* Berkeley, CA: Peachpit Printing.

McFedries, P. (1997). *The complete idiot's guide to creating an HTML 4 web page.* Indianapolis, IN: Que Education and Training.

Pedersen, T., Sloan, P. S., & Moss, F. (1998). *Make your own web page: A guide for kids.* Los Angeles: Price Stern Sloan Publishing.

Smith, B. E. (1998). *Creating web pages for dummies* (3rd ed.). San Mateo, CA: IDG Books Worldwide.

Szeto, G. (1997). *Designing interactive web sites.* Rochelle Park, NJ: Hayden Books.

Williams, R. (1997). *The non-designer's web book: An easy guide to creating, designing, and posting your own web site.* Berkeley, CA: Peachpit Printing.

Web sites

http://www.mcli.dist.maricopa.edu/authoring
Multimedia Authoring Web

http://www.sci.kun.nl/thalia/guide/index.html
Thalia: Tips and Tricks for WWW Providers

http://www.nas.nasa.gov/NAS/WebWeavers
World Wide Web tools for Aspiring Web Weavers

CHAPTER IX

Products and Competitions

After the product has been developed and evaluated, it may be a great idea to enter it into a competition. There are many benefits, including: the development of self-confidence; constructive use of time; possible recognition for your strengths, abilities, and interests; networking through meeting many people outside your school/community; and the possibility of winning scholarships, cash, trophies, ribbons, certificates, travel, and other fun prizes.

If there is an interest in participating in competitions, there are several ways to get information. Contact persons within the school, such as teachers, guidance counselor, principal, curriculum coordinator, media specialist, and others who may know of specific competitions. In some cases, local librarians may also have information on competitions. Look in magazines and newspapers for announcements about them. Write for the specific information, read the application and rules carefully for details, and always adhere to all deadlines.

There are hundreds of competitions from which to choose, depending on the type of product and the grade/age level. For visual products, the following are a few suggestions:

The Lions International Peace Poster
Lions Clubs International, 300 22nd St., Oak Brook, IL 60521-8842
Ages 11–13

U.S. Savings Bonds National Student Poster Contest
Coordinator, National Student Poster Contest, Savings Bonds Marketing Office, Department of the Treasury, Bureau of the Public Debt, Washington, DC 20226
Grades 4–6

Reflections Cultural Arts Program
The National PTA, 330 N. Wabash Ave., Ste. 2100, Chicago, IL 60611
Preschool–High school

International Student Media Festival
The Association for Educational Communications and Technology International Student Media Festival, EYECUPS-2644 Rica Road, Annapolis, MD 21401
Kindergarten–College

Reflections Scholarship Competition
The National PTA, 330 N. Wabash Ave., Ste. 2100, Chicago, IL 60611-3690
High School

Congressional Art Competition

Congressional Arts Caucus, U.S. Congress, Washington, DC 20515
Grades 9–12

National Two-Dimensional Art Contest

Frances Hook Scholarship Fund, P.O. Box 597346, Chicago, IL 60659-7346
Grades 1–12

Written products are also appropriate for competitions. Here are a few to think about:

The National Written and Illustrated By ... Awards Contest for Students

Landmark Editions Inc., P.O. Box 4469, Kansas City, MO 64127
Ages 6–19

Kids Are Authors

Trumpet Book Fairs, 801 94th Ave. N, St. Petersburg, FL 33702
Grade K–8

Ann Arlys Bowler Poetry Contest

Weekly Reader Corp., 245 Long Hill Road, Middletown, CT 06457
Grades 4–12

Mississippi Valley Poetry Contest

North American Literary Espadrille, P.O. Box 3188, Rock Island, IL 61204-3188
Elementary to Elderly

Paul A. Witty Outstanding Literature Award

International Reading Association, Texas Christian University
P.O. Box 32925, Fort Worth, TX 76129
Grade K–12

Allyn M. Caffer Memorial Short Story Writing Contest

Allyn M. Caffer Memorial Short Story Writing Contest
984 Reliefs Road, Yardley, PA 19067
Grades 7–12

Baker's Plays High School Playwriting Contest

Baker's Plays, 100 Chauncy St., Boston, MA 02111
High School

Young Playwrights Festival

Young Playwrights Inc., 321 W. 44th St., Ste. 906, New York, NY 10036
Ages 18 and younger

Annual NewsCurrents Student Editorial Cartoon Contest
Knowledge Unlimited Inc. Publisher of the Weekly
NewsCurrents Current Events Program
P.O. Box 52, Madison, WI 53701
Grades K–12

For students, who have developed oral products, these may be of interest:

National Juniors Forensic League
National Forensic League, Box 38, Ripon, WI 54971
Grades 6–9

National High School Oratorical Competition
The American Legion National Headquarters
P.O. Box 1055, Indianapolis, IN 46206-1055
High School

For performing arts competitions, the following examples may be beneficial:

The Donna Reed Foundation for the Performing Arts
The Donna Reed Foundation for the Performing Arts
Scholarship Division, P.O. Box 122, Denison, IA 51442
High School Seniors

Reflections Cultural Arts Program
The National PTA
330 N. Wabash Ave., Ste. 2100, Chicago, IL 60611
Preschool–High School

Delius Composition Contest for High School Composers
The Delius Association, College of Fine Arts, Jacksonville, FL 32211
Grades 10–12

For multi-categorical products, these may be right for you:

Duracell/NSTA Scholarship Competition
Duracell NSTA Scholarship Competition
1840 Wilson Blvd., Arlington, VA 22201-3000
Grades 9–12

Young Inventors and Creators Program
National Inventive Thinking Association, P.O. Box 836202, Richardson, TX 75083
Grades 7–12

Young Games Inventors Contest
U.S. Kids, P.O. Box 567, Indianapolis, IN 46206
Ages 13 and under

For more detailed information on more than 275 competitions please consult:

Karnes, F. A., & Riley, T. L. (1996). *Competitions: Maximizing your abilities.* Waco, TX: Prufrock Press.

CHAPTER X

Product Journal

The following pages have been provided for you to organize and reflect on your thoughts relating to product development. In addition to completing these forms, you may wish to keep a product journal or log to record additional ideas you may have.

Reflection is an important component of product development and evaluation. By writing down your thoughts, you will further enhance your product development experiences.

Additions! Additions! Additions!

The product profiles contained in this book should not be considered all-inclusive. If you discover other definitions, product types, words to know, exemplary producers, helpful hints, community resources, or quotes to inspire during your research, make note of them using the form below.

Product:

Definition:

Types:

Words to Know:

Exemplary Producers:

Helpful Hints:

Community Resources:

Quotes to Inspire:

Why I Want to
Develop & Evaluate a Product

There may be many great reasons for developing and evaluating a product. Record as many as you can now and add to your list as you think of more.

- _____
_____
_____

- _____
_____
_____

- _____
_____
_____

- _____
_____
_____

- _____
_____
_____

- _____
_____
_____

- _____
_____
_____

- _____
_____
_____

My Product Goals

What are your product goals? What skills in product development would you like to enhance? With whom would you like to meet and share your ideas? Product development can lead to the accomplishment of many personal goals. Think about your goals and how you plan to achieve them through product development. Write down your thoughts as you meet your goals, and decide on new ones.

Goal: _____

Steps to achieving my goal:

1) _____

2) _____

3) _____

4) _____

Goal: _____

Steps to achieving my goal:

1) _____

2) _____

3) _____

4) _____

My Product Calendar

Having and maintaining a schedule for developing and evaluating your product is very important. You may want to record your schedule on your computer, or perhaps you have a desk or pocket calendar.

Here's a great sample:

Day of the Week	Things to do Today
Monday	
Tuesday	
Wednesday	
Thursday	
Friday	
Saturday	
Sunday	

Materials for My Product

As you begin to think about your products, you will have to assess materials and other resources. Which materials do you have? Which ones will you need to acquire? Where will you get these materials?

Materials I Have	Materials I Need	Where to Get Them

Places I've Displayed
My Product

There are many places within your school and community to display your products. Keeping a record will help you remember the details for future exhibitions.

Product	Dates	Places

Product Selection
Why I Did What I Did!

Reflect upon the process you went through in order to select a product to develop. What elements of the following criteria contributed to your choice of product?

Interests:

Talents & Abilities:

Resources:

Other:

What I Have Learned About Myself
While Developing Products

Product development can teach you a lot of things about yourself, your interests, your strengths, and your abilities. You can learn more about your work habits, attitudes, and goals for the future as you plan your product and have fun. Through product development, I have learned the following about my:

Interests:

Strengths:

Abilities:

Attitudes:

Work Habits:

Goals:

Research Skills:

Presentation Skills:

Time Management:

The Thrill of
Developing Products!

Think about the thrill of gaining new knowledge and transforming the information into a product. How do you feel or think you will feel before, during, and after developing a product? Write the ways you feel and the reasons for those feelings.

When thinking and developing my product, I may feel or have felt _____

_____

_____

_____

_____

_____

During the development of my product, I may feel or have felt _____

_____

_____

_____

_____

_____

After completing my product, I may feel or have felt _____

_____

_____

_____

_____

_____

Things I can do in developing products in the future to make myself feel better _____

_____

_____

_____

_____

_____

Products I Would Like to Try in the Future

Keep a list of the different types of products you would like to create. Be sure to try your hand at many different kinds.

Visual:

Written:

Oral:

Performance:

Multi-Categorical:

Having Fun With Product Development Through Competitions

There are many opportunities for you to participate in competitions as discussed in Chapter IX with a few national competition examples. There are also an abundance to be found at the local, state, regional, national, and international levels. Record your options on a form similar to the one below. You may want to have a special tablet, card file, or put them on your computer.

Competition: _____

Contact Person: _____

Street Address: _____

City, State, Zip Code: _____

Date of Submittal: _____

Date of Competition: _____

Award/Prize/Recognition: _____

For more information on competitions, consult:
Karnes, F. A., & Riley, T. L. (1996). *Competitions: Maximizing your abilities*. Waco, TX: Prufrock Press.

Greatest Product Developers
Hall of Fame
NOMINATION FORM

Who would you nominate as the greatest developer of a specific product? Record your nominees below and justify your selection.

Product	Developer	Reasons for Nomination

Let Us Know About Your Product!

You and your product are important to us. We want to know about the steps in the development of your product. Let us hear from you.

I am in the _____ grade.

My product was:

- ❑ Visual
- ❑ Oral
- ❑ Written
- ❑ Performance
- ❑ Multi-Categorical

My product was a _____.

My research included the following academic area(s): _____
_____

The process skills used were: _____
_____

My organization skills used were: _____
_____

My audience(s) was (were): _____
_____

I would offer the following advice to others about product development:_____
_____

What suggestions would you have for additional information for this book? _____
_____

Other comments: _____
_____

Mail this form to:

The Center for Gifted Studies
The University of Southern Mississippi
Box 8207
Hattiesburg, MS 39406-8207